THE WORD OF WISDOM TODAY

THE WORD OF WISDOM TODAY

ROY W. DOXEY

Published by Deseret Book Company, Salt Lake City, Utah, 1975

DEDICATION

To Cherilyn
David
Debra
Daniel
and Cosette

To Valerie
Christina
Pamela
and Thomas

To Christine
Cathrine
and Carolyn

To Christopher
Bethany
and Melanie

And to future grandchildren
with love and with faith that they
will follow the example of their
parents in obeying the Word of
Wisdom so that they may live the other
commandments of the Lord

Contents

Preface

Over 140 years ago the Prophet Joseph Smith, first president of The Church of Jesus Christ of Latter-day Saints, received a revelation that is unique in the Christian world. This revelation, known as the Word of Wisdom, has been proved abundantly true as to its spiritual and temporal promises. A more remarkable document dealing with these two aspects of life would be difficult, if not impossible, to find. For many decades faithful Latter-day Saints have demonstrated its spiritual authenticity. And now we are hearing almost daily the affirmations of science, a developing system of knowledge that shall yet bring further confirmation of the eternal truths recorded in the Word of Wisdom.

There are many reasons for which this volume was written, chief of which is a sincere desire of the author to bring to all people the truths of temporal and spiritual salvation embodied in the Word of Wisdom. Special thought has been given to investigators of the Church and those who have accepted the atonement of Jesus Christ as members of his church, especially the youth, who are bombarded daily with the enticings of conspiring men to trap them in sin. The Word of Wisdom is a commandment of the Lord designed to show the way of truth, for "men are, that they might have joy." (2 Nephi 2:25.) The obedient who abide by its provisions are blessed both temporally and spiritually, and receive joy thereby. (Mosiah 2:41.) In a temporal sense, obedience brings health of body and mind; in a spiritual sense, keeping the commandments brings the blessings of the eternities. In this life we receive "hidden treasures of knowledge," which give us peace of mind and soul.

Several persons have made contributions to this volume. Acknowledgment is made with appreciation to Elder Mark E. Petersen of the Council of the Twelve for permission to use a general conference sermon in Chapter 7. Also included in that chapter is an article by Hugh J. Mooney of Rochester, New York, who expresses a powerful testimony of the dire consequences of using cigarettes. Special appreciation is given to Dr. Richard A. Call, medical director of the Utah Valley Hospital, Provo, Utah, for the use of medical publications and for many helpful suggestions on the chapters relating to medical research. Appreciation is also expressed to Evelyn Schiess for her assistance in putting together the manuscript of this volume. Last, but not least, I acknowledge with deep appreciation my wife, Alberta, for her continued encouragement and helpful suggestions in the editing process.

The philosophy of the Church is that man should enjoy a useful and productive life by living and keeping the commandments of the Lord. The gospel, in spirit and letter, enjoins upon all who desire the blessings of life here and in the future eternities to keep all the laws of Jesus Christ, an important part of which is the Word of Wisdom. It is the testimony of the author, borne of the Spirit and of experience, that the observance of this commandment and others brings rich and rewarding blessings. Blessings received over a long life of devotion to the kingdom of God deepens one's appreciation of the "hidden treasures" promised by the Divine Being who gave the revelation as well as knowledge that he is literally the resurrected Son of the Eternal Father, that he lives, and that his promises never fail.

Roy W. Doxey

A Distinctive Commandment

What is the Word of Wisdom? On February 27, 1833, the Prophet Joseph Smith received a revelation at Kirtland, Ohio, and this revelation, found in section 89 of the Doctrine and Covenants, is known to members of The Church of Jesus Christ of Latter-day Saints as the Word of Wisdom. It reads as follows:

A Word of Wisdom, for the benefit of the council of high priests, assembled in Kirtland, and the church, and also the saints in Zion—
To be sent greeting; not by commandment or constraint, but by revelation and the word of wisdom, showing forth the order and will of God in the temporal salvation of all saints in the last days—
Given for a principle with promise, adapted to the capacity of the weak and the weakest of all saints, who are or can be called saints.
Behold, verily, thus saith the Lord unto you: In consequence of evils and designs which do and will exist in the hearts of conspiring men in the last days, I have warned you, and forewarn you, by giving you this word of wisdom by revelation—
That inasmuch as any man drinketh wine or strong drink among you, behold it is not good, neither meet in the sight of your Father, only in assembling yourselves together to offer up your sacraments before him.
And, behold, this should be wine, yea, pure wine of the grape of the vine, of your own make.
And, again, strong drinks are not for the belly, but for the washing of your bodies.
And again, tobacco is not for the body, neither for the belly, and is not good for man, but is an herb for bruises and all sick cattle, to be used with judgment and skill.
And again, hot drinks are not for the body or belly.
And again, verily I say unto you, all wholesome herbs God hath ordained for the constitution, nature, and use of man—
Every herb in the season thereof, and every fruit in the season thereof; all these to be used with prudence and thanksgiving.
Yea, flesh also of beasts and of the fowls of the air, I, the Lord, have ordained for the use of man with thanksgiving;

nevertheless they are to be used sparingly;

And it is pleasing unto me that they should not be used, only in time of winter, or of cold, or famine.

All grain is ordained for the use of man and of beasts, to be the staff of life, not only for man but for the beasts of the field, and the fowls of heaven, and all wild animals that run or creep on the earth;

And these hath God made for the use of man only in times of famine and excess of hunger.

All grain is good for the food of man; as also the fruit of the vine; that which yieldeth fruit, whether in the ground or above the ground—

Nevertheless, wheat for man, and corn for the ox, and oats for the horse, and rye for the fowls and for swine, and for all beasts of the field, and barley for all useful animals, and for mild drinks, as also other grain.

And all saints who remember to keep and do these sayings, walking in obedience to the commandments, shall receive health in their navel and marrow to their bones;

And shall find wisdom and great treasures of knowledge, even hidden treasures;

And shall run and not be weary, and shall walk and not faint.

And I, the Lord, give unto them a promise, that the destroying angel shall pass by them, as the children of Israel, and not slay them. Amen.

Observance of the Word of Wisdom is a distinctive practice of Latter-day Saints. They do not claim to be the only Christians who observe health laws as a part of their religious faith, but the Word of Wisdom is distinctive with them for these reasons:

First, it is a revelation from God received by the Prophet Joseph Smith.

Second, its promises to the obedient include not only physical and mental health, but also spiritual blessings.

Third, it contains a prophetic warning, which is being literally fulfilled regarding the efforts of conspiring men to foster upon the public things detrimental to health.

Fourth, its provisions are, by and large, being substantiated by science.

It is not uncommon for members of the Church to be known for their abstinence from tobacco, alcoholic beverages, and tea and coffee. In fact, some employers have hired Latter-day Saints because of their living this law, as well as other characteristics associated with those who live the gospel and are reliable, trustworthy, and honest, and observe the laws of the land.

There are many reasons why the faithful Latter-day Saint observes this important commandment, for he understands the need to fulfill his covenant relationship with God in not only being a good example of Christian ideals, but also to lead an exemplary life, which assists in the furtherance of the work of the Lord.

Ancient Israel was scattered among the "heathen" because in their iniquity they profaned the name of God. Looking to a later period, the latter times, the prophet Ezekiel saw the time when there would be a modern house of Israel that would not profane God's name.

> But I had pity for mine holy name, which the house of Israel had profaned among the heathen, whither they went.
> Therefore say unto the house of Israel, Thus saith the Lord God; I do not this for your sakes, O house of Israel, but for mine holy name's sake, which ye have profaned among the heathen, whither ye went.
> And I will sanctify my great name, which was profaned among the heathen, which ye have profaned in the midst of them; and the heathen shall know that I am the Lord, saith the Lord God, when I shall be sanctified in you before their eyes.
> For I will take you from among the heathen, and gather you out of all countries, and will bring you into your own land. (Ezekiel 36:21-24.)

Latter-day Saints see themselves as modern Israelites, gathered out of the world into the kingdom of God to enjoy the blessings of obedience to commandments given through a modern prophet, Joseph Smith. In the early part of their history, which began when the Church of our day was organized on April 6, 1830, they gathered from many nations into areas founded by them as refuges from the world. In the early days of the Church these gathering places included Ohio, Illinois, and Missouri. From 1847 on, the great western part of the United States was their refuge, and today the Church headquarters are located in Salt Lake City, Utah. An ancient American prophet saw the time when the saints of God would also be scattered among the nations, armed with righteousness and with the power of God. (See 1 Nephi 14:14.) They are commanded to "stand in holy places," for the day would come, when circumstances warranted, that they would be counseled by proper authority to again gather into designated places. (D&C 101: 20-22.)

The "holy places" are the branches and wards of the Church; in a real sense, they are also the homes of faithful Latter-day Saints where the principles of the gospel of Jesus Christ are taught and practiced. When a member of the Church accepts fully the commandments of the Lord, including the Word of Wisdom, he contributes to the fulfillment of the Lord's words to Ezekiel: ". . . and the heathen shall know that I am the Lord, . . . when I shall be sanctified in you before their eyes." (Ezekiel 36:23.) Devout Latter-day Saints know that they show by their actions that they represent the Lord and are known to him. Appropriate to this truth is this question: Is God known to those who have not received him in a covenant relationship when they see those who do profess to follow him failing to keep his commandments? The scriptures proclaim that God is perfect in the virtues represented in the gospel of Jesus Christ. In order that he might be known to those who have not received him, his followers must demonstrate to the world that they are trying to be like him.

The title "saint" does not imply that members of The Church of Jesus Christ of Latter-day Saints are perfect, for absolute perfection does not come in mortality, but they see in this holy title one meaning—that of being set apart to the cause of God. They also see themselves as not being without blemish or blame, but striving to become as the Father and Son are. Through observance of the Word of Wisdom, Latter-day Saints let others know one of the ways in which they teach by example the gospel way of life.

One fundamental purpose for which The Church of Jesus Christ of Latter-day Saints has been restored to the earth is that it might be the means whereby the members

4

might seek for perfection. Jesus declared that perfection is necessary in order for one to attain eternal life or exaltation in God's presence. (See Matthew 5:48; 3 Nephi 12:48; Moses 1:39.) The writer of the epistle to the Hebrews encouraged the saints to strive for perfection; as the Prophet Joseph said, they should not leave the fundamental principles of the gospel, but should continue to build upon these foundation stones. (See Hebrews 6:1-3; *Teachings of the Prophet Joseph Smith,* pp. 328, 364.)

In baptism a person covenants with the Lord that he will, as the sacramental prayers state, (1) always remember the Savior, (2) take upon himself the name of Jesus Christ, and (3) always keep his commandments. These covenants require full devotion to the Savior's way of life.

The dedicated Latter-day Saint who is imbued with the Holy Spirit understands that the Lord has never given anyone the right to consider one principle of the gospel useless or unnecessary, or to decide which commandment is most important. Each principle is essential to salvation. The Lord knows that each person is different, but he knows also that each person is capable, if he diligently tries, of reaching perfection. Some may believe that it is a goal that is impossible to attain, depending upon their maturity in gospel learning and practice. In the beginning of one's life in the kingdom of God it may seem that far too many expectations are made, but as time passes and faith and conviction increase, the task becomes easier and comes closer to realization. A modern revelation on the gifts of the Holy Ghost indicates that great blessings come to those who love the Lord and keep *all* his commandments. Important to all members of the Church is the Lord's promise that he "that seeketh so to do" is acceptable of him. (D&C 46:8-9.) The Lord does not condone sin, but those who earnestly strive to overcome the barriers to their salvation by sincerely endeavoring to perfect themselves through repentance will receive the necessary help to aid them. (D&C 1:31-33.) The purpose of the gospel is to save and not to condemn, for the Lord's hand is outstretched to all who want his help. (Matthew 11:28-30.)

A unique contribution of the gospel that has special meaning to an understanding of the Word of Wisdom and all other teachings relating to earth life is given in a modern revelation:

6

> Wherefore, verily I say unto you that all things unto me are spiritual, and not at any time have I given unto you a law which was temporal; neither any man, nor the children of men; neither Adam, your father, whom I created.
>
> Behold, I gave unto him that he should be an agent unto himself; and I gave unto him commandment, but no temporal commandment gave I unto him, for my commandments are spiritual; they are not natural nor temporal, neither carnal nor sensual. (D&C 29:34-35.)

If one believes the truths in this revelation, then he has the basis for receiving great joy and happiness. The daily acts of life become meaningful and purposeful. The gospel of Jesus Christ received through the prophets takes on new meaning. It becomes one whole plan; though it consists of many parts, all of them are unified and one in substance— spiritual.

God is concerned about our daily lives and what we do, and he gives help and assistance in our journey through mortality. He and his Son Jesus Christ are concerned be- cause we are the begotten sons and daughters of the Father, and Jesus gave his life that we might enjoy eternal life if we are obedient to the laws of the gospel. (See D&C 76:22-24; John 3:16.) God is not far from us, for by his spirit he com- munes with us, and we commune with him by the same spirit.

At no time has the Lord given a solely temporal com- mandment. All things unto the Lord are spiritual and have a spiritual meaning in our lives as we give obedience to them. President Joseph F. Smith said, concerning this sub- ject:

> You must continue to bear in mind that the temporal and the spiritual are blended. They are not separate. One cannot be carried on without the other, so long as we are here in mortality.
>
> . . . The work that we are engaged in is not designed to be

limited by the spiritual necessities of the people alone. It is the purpose of God in restoring the gospel and the Holy Priesthood not only to benefit mankind spiritually, but to benefit them temporally. (*Gospel Doctrine*, pp. 208-209.)

Is the Word of Wisdom a temporal law? Yes, in the sense that it pertains to our physical well-being. It is a practical message from the Lord designed to give bodily and spiritual vigor, for "the temporal salvation of the saints in the last days." (D&C 89:2.) The Lord uses this language so that we might, in our sphere, understand a purpose for such a law; yet all things are spiritual, and at no time is there a law that is temporal only. Is the Word of Wisdom a spiritual law? Yes! If we choose, we may refer to it as a temporal-spiritual law.

Another reason for the Word of Wisdom being known as a temporal law is the difference that may exist in our minds between the temporal and the spiritual. Without the understanding of the temporal-spiritual principle mentioned above, the temporal law would seem to be of less importance.

John A. and Leah D. Widtsoe wrote:

A person who cannot obey a temporal law, such as the Word of Wisdom, seldom can obey spiritual laws, which reach more profoundly into the nature of man. That is, those who are living the high spiritual laws of the Gospel, true saints, must have achieved sufficient desire and power of will to obey the temporal commandment known as the Word of Wisdom. Unless they have done so, the spiritual integrity of such persons may be called into question. (*The Word of Wisdom, A Modern Interpretation*, rev. ed., p. 21.)

President Stephen L Richards, first counselor in the First Presidency (1951-59), said that "the largest measure of good derived from its observance is in increased faith and the development of more spiritual power and wisdom. Likewise, the most regrettable and damaging effects of its infractions are spiritual also." (*Conference Report*, April 1949, p. 141.)

Thus we see that the Word of Wisdom, a revelation given in the beginning of the dispensation of the fulness of times, is distinctive to the Latter-day Saints because it is a program for the spiritual and temporal welfare of the last days. Latter-day Saints are under covenant to build the kingdom of God on earth, one means of which is to exemplify the principles of the gospel in their lives, and one of these principles is the Word of Wisdom. This divine law is particularly adapted to making known to the world how Latter-day Saints represent the Lord, whose plan is that his children who covenant with him should seek perfection with all their hearts. This procedure is to accept all gospel teachings, so that one's quest for exaltation might be possible.

2

History of
the Word of Wisdom

President Joseph Fielding Smith, tenth president of The Church of Jesus Christ of Latter-day Saints, related two conversations he had following a stake conference he had addressed while serving as a member of the Council of the Twelve Apostles.

> I attended a stake conference a number of years ago and spoke on the Word of Wisdom. At the close of the conference a good sister came up somewhat excited and said: "Brother Smith, you never said a word about backbiters and fault-finders, and I think it is far worse to bear false witness and to backbite than it is to drink a cup of tea."
>
> I said: "I think I can say things just as emphatic perhaps about backbiters as I can about people who break the Word of Wisdom, but I did not have that for a subject this afternoon."
>
> When I went to the rear of the building nearly everybody had left, but a man held out his hand and said:
>
> "Brother Smith, that is the first discourse on the Word of Wisdom that I ever liked."
>
> I said: "Haven't you heard other discourses on the Word of Wisdom?"
>
> He said: "Yes, but this is the first one that I ever enjoyed."
>
> I said: "How is that?"
>
> He said: "Well, you see, I am keeping the Word of Wisdom now." (*Conference Report,* October 1935, p. 12.)

What is there about the Word of Wisdom that some people find it difficult to obey? There are many answers to this question, and it is not our intention to list them all. However, it is a fact that this law is a stumbling block for many people. Addiction to a habit contrary to the Word of Wisdom may become so fixed that the physical and moral strength required to forsake the habit is sometimes considerable. Many people believe in the fulness of the gospel but an old habit keeps them from observing it fully. Others feel that since the revelation is a temporal law, it is not really important; they rationalize that it is a small matter to imbibe a drug-addictive drink when there are more important parts to the gospel of Jesus Christ. However, conversion to this principle is just as necessary as to other principles of the gospel. The key to living any teaching of the gospel is true conversion to the fulness of truth, not to parts only. Covenant relationship with God and his Son requires acceptance and living fully the teachings of the Church. Those who abide by gospel standards feel comfortable and enjoy clear consciences because the Spirit of the Lord is with them.

At all times since the Word of Wisdom was given in 1833, there have been members of the Church who have not abstained from alcoholic beverages, tobacco, tea, and coffee. In the days of the Prophet Joseph Smith many Saints were addicted to tobacco, and the use of coffee and tea was fairly common. The use of tobacco by some of the brethren in meetings was a most distasteful practice that created not only a smoke haze but also tobacco spittle on the floor. President Brigham Young related the circumstances that brought forth the Prophet's inquiry of the Lord regarding these matters.

I think I am as well acquainted with the circumstances which led to the giving of the Word of Wisdom as any man in the Church, although I was not present at the time to witness them. The first school of the prophets was held in a small room situated over the Prophet Joseph's kitchen, in a house, which belonged to Bishop [Newel K.] Whitney, and which was attached to his store, which store probably might be about fifteen feet square. In the rear of this building was a kitchen, probably ten by fourteen feet, containing rooms and pantries. Over this kitchen was situated the room in which the Prophet received revelations and in which he instructed his brethren. The brethren came to that place for hundreds of miles to attend school in a little room probably no larger than eleven by fourteen. When they assembled together in this room after breakfast, the first they did was to light their pipes, and, while smoking, talk about the great things of the kingdom, and spit all over the room, and as soon as the pipe was out of their mouths a large chew of tobacco would then be taken. Often when the Prophet entered the room to give the school instructions he would find himself in a cloud of tobacco smoke. This, and the complaints of his wife at having to clean so filthy a floor, made the Prophet think upon the matter, and he inquired of the Lord relating to the conduct of the Elders in using tobacco, and the revelation known as the Word of Wisdom was the result of his inquiry. (*Journal of Discourses,* 12:158, February 8, 1868.)

The revelations in the Doctrine and Covenants were received generally as a result of inquiry by the Prophet. The receiving of this revelation is an example of his practice in meeting specific problems. The problem was present—the use of tobacco—and one can imagine him inquiring about its use only, but the Lord gave very much more than expected, a code of laws that have stood the test of time, the revelation found in section 89 of the Doctrine and Covenants. This revelation, with all others, gives Latter-day Saints reason to look to the present prophet for the solution of problems of the day, for individuals and the Church as a whole.

11

Following the martyrdom of the Prophet and his brother Hyrum in Carthage, Illinois, on June 27, 1844, the Church moved into the western part of the United States. During this pioneer period men, women, and children suffered great hardships. Often there was insufficient food and clothing to make life comfortable, and sometimes hardly enough to sustain life. Home remedies were used for the sick, and oftentimes whiskey was used for medicinal and other purposes. The hard pioneer life required the use of things considered helpful under the circumstances and according to what was then known about cures for sicknesses.

When the Word of Wisdom was first given, many considered that it was not binding upon them, that it was given "not by commandment or constraint, but by revelation. . . ." (Verse 2.) Constraint, force, or compulsion was not to be used. Why did the Lord give this important revelation without the force of a commandment? He has not specifically given the answer to this question, but there have been some persons who have suggested an answer. President Joseph F. Smith, sixth president of the Church, gave the following:

The reason undoubtedly why the Word of Wisdom was

given—as not by "commandment or constraint" was that at that time, at least, if it had been given as a commandment it would have brought every man, addicted to the use of these noxious things, under condemnation; so the Lord was merciful and gave them a chance to overcome, before he brought them under the law. (*Conference Report,* October 1913, p. 14.)

12

"Before he brought them under the law." Latter-day Saints are now under the law or commandment to observe the Word of Wisdom. In the days of President Brigham Young this revelation became binding upon the Saints. Recognizing that many did not observe this law, he said:

Why not govern and control the appetite, that it may be subject to the law of Christ? But how is it? Why, "I must have some tobacco, if I am damned for it." Or, "I must have a cup of tea, if I am damned for it." Or, "I must have this or that, if I should have to go to hell for it." It is like saying to our Heavenly Father, "I will not mind you, I will not obey your commandments, but I will have my own way and follow the bent of my own inclinations; my appetite shall be nursed and pampered, though it be at the expense of your displeasure." Instead of pursuing this course, listen to that Spirit God has given to all, which teaches the right and how to avoid the wrong, and say to appetite, to disposition, to temper, to the whole man, you must do as I command you; I am an officer, a general in the army of Christ and I will be obeyed. (*Journal of Discourses,* 9:257, March 16, 1862.)

Many years after President Young declared that the Spirit of the Lord had told him to declare the Word of Wisdom as a commandment, Elder Francis M. Lyman of the Council of the Twelve said:

I remember so distinctly, and, no doubt, many in this congregation remember the same, when President Brigham Young, speaking as the mouthpiece of the Lord, announced, from this stand, that from that time forth the Word of Wisdom was a commandment, binding upon all Latter-day Saints. (*Conference Report,* October 1908, p. 55.)

Elder Brigham Young, Jr., in 1894 said essentially the same thing and asked this question, "Does anyone remember hearing those words from this stand more than twenty years ago?" (*Millennial Star,* 57:82, February 7, 1895.)

Consistent with what has been said regarding "commandment and constraint" and the bringing the members of the Church under this law, Elder Ezra T. Benson, an apostle of this dispensation, said on April 7, 1867:

> And let us all endeavour by the help of God to leave off our tea, coffee, liquor, and other things, that are neither good for the body nor for the belly. We can overcome, for God will not require more of us than we can do. He has borne with us these many years; but, if I can discern the signs of the times, He is now going to require these things at our hands. Supposing He had given the Word of Wisdom as a command, how many of us would have been here? I do not know; but He gave this without command or restraint, observing that it would be pleasing in His sight for His people to obey its precepts. Ought we not to try to please our Heavenly Father . . . ? (*Journal of Discourses,* 11:367, April 7, 1867.)

13

Those who pleased their Heavenly Father received rich blessings. One of these, Elder George Q. Cannon, gave his testimony:

> I never drank tea or coffee in my life, I never drank liquor, I never used tobacco, and I have endeavored to keep the Word of Wisdom. . . . I proclaim to you Latter-day Saints, that the Word of Wisdom is the word of God, that those who obey it will receive every blessing which is promised in the revelation, that they will have health, and that they will have power and blessings which they cannot conceive of until they try it. (*Journal of Discourses,* 22:105-106, July 25, 1880.)

At the next general conference, when John Taylor became the third president of the Church, George Q. Cannon was sustained as a member of the First Presidency. A matter of business was presented at that conference that should set at rest any idea as to whether or not the Word of Wisdom is a commandment, binding upon the membership of the Church. Some deletions and additions had been made in the Doctrine and Covenants and the Pearl of Great Price; consequently it was felt that these new editions be approved by the membership of the Church. President Cannon held in his hands before the conference these two standard works of the Church and declared: ". . . it has been deemed wise to submit these books with their contents to the conference, to see whether the conference will vote *to accept the books and their contents as from God, and binding upon us as a people and as a Church.*" President Joseph F. Smith seconded the motion, and the conference sustained the proposition by unanimous vote. (*Journal History*, October 10, 1880.)

3

The Order and Will of the Lord

As one reads the revelation on the Word of Wisdom, he sees that though it was given not by commandment or constraint, the Lord expects' his covenant people to live its provisions. As we have seen, they would not be under condemnation as if they had disobeyed a commandment; on the other hand, however, they will not receive the blessings that obedience to that revelation promises them. The words of the Lord are explicit regarding obedience: "There is a law, irrevocably decreed in heaven before the foundations of this world, upon which all blessings are predicated—And when we obtain any blessing from God, it is by obedience to that law upon which it is predicated." (D&C 130:20-21.)

Another truth given in modern revelations is just as definite: "I, the Lord, am bound when ye do what I say; but when ye do not what I say, ye have no promise." (D&C 82:10.)

The revelation was addressed not only to the "council of high priests," but to the "church, and also the saints in Zion." (D&C 89:1.) Furthermore, it was for the temporal salvation of all saints in the last days. (Verse 2.) Clearly, this revelation was intended for all saints, "adapted to the capacity of the weak and the weakest of all saints, who are or can be called saints." (Verse 3.)

With these truths clearly stated regarding obedience to the Word of Wisdom, and in view of the fact that some of the Latter-day Saints did not wholeheartedly accept this law as binding upon them, why was it left for another generation to live the plan? We have already seen from President Joseph F. Smith that if the Word of Wisdom had been given as a commandment in the beginning, it would have brought under condemnation those who are addicted to harmful things. In addition, two other reasons for another generation being given the commandment seem plausible: (1) a new generation has a better opportunity to acquire habits consistent with gospel standards; and (2) as the tempo of world events increases toward a complete fulfillment of prophecies preceding the second coming of Christ, there is a greater need for increased missionary work.

16

Youth of a new generation have a much better opportunity to shape their lives than do those who have already acquired habits that militate against their well-being. The Lord, therefore, gave this counsel anciently and in a modern revelation:

> Seek ye the Lord while he may be found, call upon him while he is near. (Isaiah 55:6.)
>
> Train up a child in the way he should go; and when he is old, he will not depart from it. (Proverbs 22:6.)
>
> ...behold, I come quickly, and my reward is with me, and they who have sought me early shall find rest to their souls. Even so. Amen. (D&C 54:10.)
>
> He that seeketh me early shall find me, and shall not be forsaken. (D&C 88:83.)

There are advantages in coming to the Lord early. The young learn fast and are easily influenced, and especially is this necessary in setting proper habits; one's education in gospel principles over a long period of time brings many more opportunities for service in the kingdom of God; and over a longer period of time one may build up sufficient spiritual strength to overcome temptations. We build a reservoir of strength by keeping the commandments of our Father in heaven.

Although these scriptures emphasize that one should come to the Lord early in life, he who comes late in life, regardless of his age, is also acceptable to the Lord. Regardless of when a person comes, he is the subject of salvation; nevertheless, if the opportunity comes early in life, so much the better for the individual who sincerely accepts his opportunities for soul growth.

The dispensation of the fulness of times is the culminating period of God's work when all the dispensations of the gospel are brought into one complete period.

(See Acts 3:18-21; Ephesians 1:9-10.) During this time the world will see fulfilled the purpose for the establishment of the Lord's church for the last time—to prepare for the second coming of Christ, which will inaugurate his millennial reign when greater opportunities might be spent in bringing salvation to the dead who did not have the privilege in this life of receiving the gospel.

17

The Lord has placed upon his church the responsibility for warning the world, that they may not only be saved from the destructions of the last days, but also (and even more important) that they may receive blessings in this life and in the life to come. In the beginning of this dispensation the call went forth for missionaries to engage in making the gospel message known. Great numbers went forward to proclaim the glad tidings; though their opportunities in terms of availability of missionary helps, communication, and transportation were not as good as may be found today, their efforts helped the kingdom grow and brought great rewards to themselves. Surely, this is "the eleventh hour, and the last time that I shall call laborers into my vineyard." (D&C 33:3.)

Those who observe world conditions today are keenly aware of increased wickedness, the loss of peace, and the progressive fulfillment of other prophecies regarding the imminence of the Lord's coming. Thus the leaders of the Church are increasing their efforts in calling more missionaries and making it possible for the gospel message to be brought to greater numbers. Modern inventions are being used to a greater extent in this program.

Foreseeing events as they are and will be, the Lord has given the Church a period of time in which to come closer to perfection in living the gospel standards. Not only are formally called missionaries responsible for teaching the gospel, but *every* member is expected to be a missionary. How best may a member prepare for a formal mission call or to be a missionary in his own calling? By living the principles of the gospel! Observance of the Word of Wisdom is a real missionary tool in a day when the principles of this law are disregarded by the world. Latter-day Saints demonstrate its principles before the eyes of the nonbeliever. Might this be one important reason accounting for a later generation's coming under the force of commandment?

18

Admittedly, some Latter-day Saints do not represent the Lord because they do not keep the commandments, including the Word of Wisdom. The parable of the ten virgins, which was given by the Lord in his mortal ministry and reiterated in this dispensation, tells of five virgins who were prepared to meet the bridegroom while the remaining five were unprepared. The unprepared were not allowed to enter the marriage feast, which symbolized the kingdom of heaven. The Savior said: "Verily I say unto you, I know you not. Watch therefore, for ye know neither the day nor the hour wherein the Son of Man cometh." (Matthew 25:12-13.) Does this parable apply to the Latter-day Saints? A modern revelation plainly makes the answer perfectly clear that it does. (See D&C 45:56-59.)

Today we stand under divine edict to so live that we shall demonstrate to the world that we truly represent the Lord. This mission is a part of the covenant we receive when we commit ourselves to take his name upon us in the waters of baptism. (See D&C 20:37.)

Section 89 of the Doctrine and Covenants is a revelation from God. Should one ignore his counsel to his people? Is it necessary that he command in all things? In July 1831, a revelation was received by Joseph Smith in which the Lord gives counsel to be applied to Saints everywhere: (1) They are not to be commanded in all things; (2) they must use initiative; (3) they have power within themselves to do much good; and (4) God's promises may be revoked if his commandments are not obeyed. (See D&C 58:26-32.) An underlying principle in these verses is man's free agency. He must exercise his right of choice; consequently, the Lord used the word "constraint" in reference to the Word of Wisdom. (D&C 89:2.) Elder James E. Talmage, an apostle of the dispensation, observed:

> The predominant attribute of justice, recognized as part of the divine nature, forbids the thought that man should receive

promises of reward of righteousness, and threats of punishment for evil deeds, if he possessed no power of independent action. It is no more a part of God's plan to compel men to work righteousness than it is His purpose to permit evil powers to force His children to sin. . . . (*The Articles of Faith,* p. 53.)

Why should a person be compelled in all things if he has free agency? He grows by exercising his right to solve his own problems; growth would stop if he were to act as a robot. Thus the Lord provides guidance so that our journey to eternal life might be sure. Divine guidance eliminates the need to waste time and energy.

One of the early commandments given, even before the Church was organized, was to work for the establishment of Zion on the earth. (See D&C 6:6.) Inasmuch as this goal is for all Latter-day Saints, anything that we do to advance the interests of the kingdom of God redounds to our happiness here and forever.

Is the will of God any less important to us than is a commandment? If one is a slothful servant who does nothing until he is commanded and who receives the Lord's word with a doubting heart, is it not consistent, as the Lord said, that he shall be damned and receive no reward?

President Heber J. Grant gave this answer to a question about the Word of Wisdom:

I have heard any number of Latter-day Saints say, "Why, the Word of Wisdom is not a commandment."
What does the Word of Wisdom say? That it is the mind and the will of the Lord. (*Gospel Standards,* Improvement Era, 1969, p.54.)

Elder George F. Richards said on the subject of the Word of Wisdom being the order and will of God:

We have accepted Joseph Smith as the prophet, seer, and revelator of this last dispensation, and in doing so we accept these revelations as being the word of the Lord to us. Here the Lord expresses His *will,* in very plain terms, that this revelation is given "showing forth the *order* and *will* of God." If for no other reason, this should be sufficient for any consistent Latter-day Saint to induce him to yield implicit obedience unto this word. I can think of no gospel subject that will apply directly to more people among us as Latter-day Saints than this Word of Wisdom, unless it may be the principle of obedience, which includes yielding obedience unto this word; or repentance, which also includes turning away from these things which are forbidden, and obeying the will of the Lord. (*Conference Report,* October 1908, pp. 87-88.)

20   After reading the foregoing, can you see the difference between the will of the Lord and a commandment? In the Sermon on the Mount the Savior said: "Not every one that saith unto me, Lord, Lord, shall enter into the kingdom of heaven; but he that doeth the *will* of my Father which is in heaven." (Matthew 7:21. Italics added.)

Continuing his discourse, Elder Richards said that since perfection is the goal of the gospel, "we never can reach perfection until we yield obedience unto this simple word of the Lord."

We are required to do the will of God, at any sacrifice. I have in mind the word of the Lord upon this subject, contained in the revelations: "Let no man be afraid to lay down his life for my sake; for whoso layeth down his life for my sake, shall find it again, and whoso is not willing to lay down his life for my sake is not my disciple." [D&C 103:27-28.] We are not asked now . . . to lay down our lives to show our obedience to the Lord, and our worthiness to be His disciples, but we are asked by the Lord to abstain from the use of strong drinks and tobacco, in every form, also to abstain from the use of meats to excess. This is a simple requirement. How can we hope to have faith to lay down our lives, how can we claim to be willing to do so, while our lives and actions every day, show to our neighbors and to the Lord that we are not willing to rid ourselves of the use of strong drink or tobacco—those things which are forbidden of the Lord? Let us be consistent with ourselves and our professions of faith. (Ibid., p. 88.)

"We are required to do the will of God, at any sacrifice." The faith and understanding of Nephi, Book of Mormon prophet, is well known to Latter-day Saints who have tested this principle: "I will go and do the things which the Lord hath commanded, for I know that the Lord giveth no commandments unto the children of men, save he shall prepare a way for them that they may accomplish the thing which he commandeth them." (1 Nephi 3:7.)

Sometimes laws are given to test the faith of the people.

One such case was the commandment to Abraham that he slay Isaac. (See Genesis 22.) This case illustrates what is necessary for all who seek eternal life, as declared by the Prophet Joseph Smith: "The sacrifice required of Abraham in the offering up of Isaac, shows that if a man would attain to the keys of the kingdom of an endless life; he must sacrifice all things. When God offers a blessing or knowledge to a man, and he refuses to receive it, he will be damned." (*Teachings of the Prophet Joseph Smith*, p. 322.)

21

Sacrifice, which is required of all those who want to achieve the highest degree of salvation, is earned by proving that we are willing to obey the Lord regardless of the circumstances. Can it be truthfully said that in giving up habits contrary to the Word of Wisdom, one is sacrificing, in view of the rewards held out by the Lord for such action? Without such knowledge of present and eternal rewards, to one who lacks faith in Christ it probably would seem a great sacrifice; yet, to the informed, is it?

"Therefore, O ye that embark in the service of God, see that ye serve him with all your heart, might, mind and strength, that ye may stand blameless before God at the last day." (D&C 4:2.)

4

Conspiring Men in the Last Days

I want to raise a warning voice to the members of the Church, and especially to the youth of the Church. Do not pay heed to the wicked and malicious advertising of tobacco nor of liquor. The advertising of tobacco today is one of the greatest offenses and crimes before our Father in heaven, and those who are guilty of it will one day have to pay the price. They do it now because of greed, but we must not listen to these enticings and to the wicked advertising of things that are detrimental to the body and condemned by our Father in heaven and his Son Jesus Christ, contrary to the gospel they have given to us. (Joseph Fielding Smith, *Conference Report*, October 1960, p. 51.)

A principal purpose of prophecy is to warn of impending judgments so that people might have an opportunity to repent before calamities come upon them. To prophesy is one of the minor functions of a prophet. Nonetheless, Joseph Smith was blessed richly with the prophetic gift. From the Doctrine and Covenants alone one finds great numbers of prophetic statements that have been or are in progress of fulfillment. The test of a prophecy is whether or not it is fulfilled. (See Deuteronomy 18:21-22.)

Although the following verse is not stated in the usual form of a prophecy, the prophetic element in it is clear: "Behold, verily, thus saith the Lord unto you: In consequence of evils and designs which do and will exist in the hearts of conspiring men in the last days, I have warned you, and forewarn you, by giving unto you this word of wisdom by revelation." (D&C 89:4.)

A primary purpose for which this revelation was given was because of the prophesied efforts of conspiring men to deceive people in regard to food and drink. It is also true that matters relating to the living of this law are of such importance that one's spiritual welfare is affected by obedience to it.

This prophecy applies not only to the matters revealed in the revelation, but also to the exercise of wisdom by a

Latter-day Saint that he will strive to keep *all* of the Lord's commandments. Elder Delbert L. Stapley of the Council of the Twelve declared:

> I repeat, this warning concerning the evils and designs of conspiring men, although given in the revelation on the Word of Wisdom, has a much broader application than normally applied to its forbidden items, and, if rightly viewed, encompasses every field of human endeavor. It is equally true that the use of the things forbidden in the Word of Wisdom also serve[s] to break down the accepted Christian virtues and moral concepts of life which so often lead to other more serious transgressions and sins. To narrow the meaning of this warning would make us vulnerable to the wicked designs of conspiring men who are not interested in the salvation of man but rather are interested in their own personal favor or gain. The Savior gave warning that in these last days Satan will rage in the hearts of the children of men and will stir them up to anger against that which is good.
>
> "And others," said the great American prophet, Nephi, "will he pacify, and lull them away into carnal security, that they will say: All is well in Zion; yea, Zion prospereth, all is well—and thus the devil cheateth their souls and leadeth them away carefully down to hell." (2 Nephi 28:21.)
>
> We cannot with safety say, "all is well in Zion." We cannot afford to become complacent and indifferent to the wicked and deceptive designs of the conspiring men. Lehi taught, "For it must needs be, that there is an opposition in all things." (*Ibid.*, 2:11.) That opposition is present in force today. The pressure of Satan's power is intensified as the time of the Savior's second coming to earth draws near. (*Conference Report*, October 1961, p. 21.)

We have previously stated that all commandments— even those that appear to be temporal—are spiritual. In the case of the Word of Wisdom, the temporal or physical benefits derived from following its provisions are apparent to the informed. Desisting from using alcoholic beverages, tobacco, tea, and coffee clearly pertains to the health of the body—an indication of the "temporal salvation" in the revelation. In subsequent chapters we will discuss some of the scientific reasons for living the Word of Wisdom, but for the present purpose it should be assumed that practices contrary to that law are injurious.

Unique in the restored gospel of Jesus Christ is emphasis upon the Lord's concern for his children, not only for their salvation in the world to come, but also for their life in mortality. Although we are expected to use our initiative in working out our problems in earth life, the Lord is also mindful of our welfare. We are spirit children of God, and this earth experience is designed to train our spirits and bodies for an eternal home. Our every need is important, and our problems, whether physical, mental, economic, or social, are of concern to the Church. It is our purpose in life to work out our salvation; therefore, the Lord's concern is for all aspects of our lives, here and in the eternities.

When we understand this basic philosophy, we can better appreciate why the Lord would give a revelation concerning our temporal and spiritual health. It is even more understandable that a revelation would contain a warning against conspiring men, if conditions were to exist that would militate against our well-being.

The desire for riches has been the cause of more crimes than probably any other single factor. Men have risked dishonor, imprisonment, loss of employment, and even death for the love of what money can bring them. The apostle Paul decried the effect that riches had upon some early members of the church in his condemnation of the love of money:

> But they that will be rich fall into temptation and a snare, and into many foolish and hurtful lusts, which drown men in destruction and perdition.
> *For the love of money is the root of all evil*: which some coveted after, they have erred from the faith, and pierced themselves through with many sorrows. (1 Timothy 6:9-10. Italics added.)

Whenever a person places anything above the purpose for which he is in life, that thing becomes his god. The love of money stands high among the gods of men. The prophet Nephi pronounced a woe upon those whose "hearts are upon their treasures; wherefore, their treasure is their God. And behold, their treasure shall perish with them also." (2 Nephi 9:30.)

Through the use of vast sums of money, the skills of

propagandists, and the determined desires of men to change people's minds toward a movement or a product, though detrimental to the well-being of a people, success may be achieved. The love of money and what it can bring has taken hold of men's minds to the degree that they are not concerned with those whose health might be impaired nor the degrading effects of their efforts.

25

Past experience and present efforts to foster upon the American public products that are injurious to health bear out the progressive fulfillment of the prophetic warning given by the Lord almost a century and a half ago.

Temperance societies were organized in the United States early in the nineteenth century to combat the evils of liquor, so that young and old might not fall victims to these evils. Later, legal means were encouraged by the temperance movement when Maine became the first state to outlaw liquor traffic in 1851, followed by a few other states. By 1919, thirty-three states had adopted prohibition laws, and national prohibition laws were put into effect in June 1919, with the Eighteenth Amendment becoming a part of the United States Constitution on January 16, 1920.

One writer gave the following reasons for the enactment of prohibition laws: (1) moral purpose—the drunkard sinned against himself, his family, his neighbors, and his God; (2) popular interest in health and physical prowess; (3) mass production in industry, which required that workers be sober; (4) the increasing social burden of the liquor traffic because of physical wrongs thrust upon some segments of society by its use; and (5) an aroused citizenry incensed by the efforts of the liquor traffic for political entrenchment. One noted citizen who was not a prohibitionist said that prohibition came not so much because of what the drys did as because of what the liquor traffic was. (Norma C. Brown, *The Alcohol Question*, Cincinnati: Standard Publishing Co., 1943, pp. 62-63.)

President Heber J. Grant made repeated appeals to the members of the Church to work for and support prohibition. After the Eighteenth Amendment was repealed in 1933 with the adoption of the Twenty-first Amendment, he said:

With the help of the Lord, to the very best of my ability, I warned this people not to vote for the repeal of the Eighteenth Amendment. I warned them against lies that were being circulated to the effect that there was more drunkenness and more use of liquor than there had been when we did not have Prohibition. Millions of dollars of money, I am sure, were expended to have the Eighteenth Amendment repealed. (*Conference Report*, April 1937, p. 13.)

26

I tell you that no greater crime was ever committed than the repealing of the Prohibition law. Billions of dollars squandered, and poverty, and heartaches, and death and damnation to many men, have come because of liquor. (*Conference Report*, October 1941, p. 147.)

The crusade against the Eighteenth Amendment illustrates well the truth of what the Lord had revealed and what his servant, the prophet and president of the Church, maintained. Fletcher Dobyns, author of a widely quoted book on the subject of repeal referred to the Association Against the Prohibition Amendment (AAPA) as the wrecking crew of the Eighteenth Amendment. He reported that Congressman Louis C. Cramton, addressing the U.S. House of Representatives on January 21, 1924, said:

This day there meets in Washington the Association Against the Prohibition Amendment in a so-called face-the-facts conference. I would, therefore, call attention at this opportune time to some facts deserving consideration in connection with that association which has in its aims, its policies and its methods more possibilities of evil for the future political, industrial, and moral welfare of our land than any other organization now in existence. It is an organization opposed to law enforcement, promoting, thriving upon and rejoicing at triumph of crime and disorder over law and order.

From its very beginning, the Association Against the Prohibition Amendment has proclaimed its nullification program. In its prospectus issued soon after the incorporation of the organization in April 1919, *before the wartime prohibition measure had gone into effect*, but some months after the Eighteenth Amendment had been ratified in the manner prescribed by the Constitution it declared:

"This association has two immediate aims: (1) To prevent the country from going on a bone-dry basis on July 1, and (2) to make the Eighteenth Amendment forever inoperative."

It daily prophesies failure, justifies violation of the law, opposes enforcement, throws its influence on the side of lawlessness when it ought to be on the side of law and order.

The leader in the whole movement to discredit the law and make it "inoperative," as originally promised by it, is the Association Against the Prohibition Amendment. (Dobyns, *The Amazing Story of Repeal*, Chicago: Willett, Clark & Company, 1940, p. 3.)

27

After declaring that the foregoing was an exact statement regarding the AAPA, Dr. Dobyns wrote:

The statement was also profoundly prophetic of the corrupting influence the organization was to exert upon the political and moral life of the nation. . . .

The motives and methods of the men behind this organization were well understood by those acquainted with the facts and were repeatedly and authoritatively exposed. But in 1930, the sinister character of the campaign they were conducting was established beyond reasonable doubt by direct and unimpeachable evidence—their own secret files, which were seized by the Senate Lobby Investigation Committee. (Ibid., pp. 3-4.)

The truth derived from evidence, "profoundly prophetic of the corrupting influence . . . upon the political and moral life of the nation," verifies the Lord's revelation made over one hundred years before Mr. Dobyns' findings! Well might one ask, What think you of the Prophet Joseph Smith? And of one of his successors, President Heber J. Grant?

The AAPA concealed its real motives by claiming that its purpose was to save the Constitution of the United States. The technique of propaganda developed during World War I was employed to the highest degree. Members of the association controlled the policy of a number of powerful daily newspapers and widely read magazines and, in addition, had ample funds to deceive the public. The following paragraph details the nefarious techniques employed to sell their designs:

When the great propaganda machine, complete in every detail and perfectly lubricated, went into action, it was a marvel of efficiency. Governor Pinchot has said that the wet propaganda covered the nation like a blanket. It would be more accurate to compare it to a bombardment. For seven years without ceasing, false and inflammatory statements were used with devastating effectiveness to destroy the intellectual and spiritual defenses against the liquor traffic that had been built up in the minds and hearts of the American people by generations of education. The social pressure, financial coercion, political corruption, lawlessness and sabotage exercised by the repeal forces were protected by an impenetrable smoke screen of fakes and falsehoods. Future generations will be able to gain only the faintest conception of the manner in which the truth was distorted. Reading the files of newspapers and magazines cannot reproduce the quality of the propaganda that was constantly pouring from the radio and from the lips of subsidized politicians, the nightly glorification of drinking by the movies, and the manner in which millions of people, having no personal knowledge of the facts, were induced to take up the catch phrases that were put in circulation to make rational thought and action impossible. (Ibid., 209-210.)

28

A group of multimillionaires who were in control of the AAPA believed that their financial interests would be greatly enhanced by repeal. One such individual said that his companies would save ten million dollars annually if the sale of beer were legalized. The association circularized heavy corporation taxpayers so that working men and others would be willing to pay a tax of three cents per glass and thus eliminate the federal corporation and income tax. (Deets Pickett, *Some Notes on the Alcohol Problem*, New York: Abingdon-Cokesbury Press, 1947, p. 91.) Every one of the AAPA's claims of benefits that would result from repeal of prohibition failed to materialize. Eleven such claims, including the reduction of drinking, decreased crime, and the safeguarding of American youth, were promises that were not fulfilled. (Brown, *The Alcohol Question*, pp. 89-93.)

Fred D. L. Squires, experienced reporter, noted the following admonitions and exhortations offered to the tradesmen of the wine industry convention heard in Chicago, Illinois, March 7-15, 1935:

"Teach American Women how to drink. . . . Invite and welcome them to your bars and taprooms.

"Show young people how to enjoy the delightful wines of America."

"We need to understand the habits of women and the younger generation. . . . Train your publicity to catch the eye and develop the interest of the younger generation."

"Make youth liquor-conscious. . . . Make it smart to drink wine."

"The liquor industry should go on the radio with up-to-date programs, with feature stars and snappy scripts, identified with prominent names."

"Nothing counts like making a profit." (Pickett, *Some Notes on the Alcohol Problem*, pp. 100-102.)

Research on the effects of smoking cigarettes was begun only a few decades ago. Increasingly, responsible scientists have charged cigarette smoking as a cause of lung cancer and other diseases. This effect was made known to the Saints on February 27, 1833, when the Lord revealed: ". . . tobacco is not for the body, neither for the belly, and is not good for man. . . ." (D&C 89:8.)

With varying degrees of acceptance and skepticism by some eminent authorities that cigarette smoking is injurious, especially as a cause of lung cancer, there has been sufficient evidence for tobacco companies to be deeply concerned about their lucrative business. As evidence against cigarettes has mounted, they have attempted to persuade the public that their products are not injurious to health.

Latter-day evidence that substantiates the prophetic utterances of the Prophet Joseph Smith regarding the evil designs of conspiring men is the record of the tobacco companies in their efforts to forestall continued loss of revenue to their businesses. On February 20, 1958, the House of Representatives Committee on Government Operations submitted to the Speaker of the House the report of its subcommittee, titled "False and Misleading Advertising (Filter-tip Cigarettes)."

With the introduction of the filter-tip cigarette, backed up by a tremendous advertising campaign, sales of such cigarettes climbed steadily while sales of regular cigarettes declined. Following the hearing of testimony for and against cigarette smoking's having a causal relationship with lung cancer, the committee turned its attention to the

sales and advertising of filter-tip cigarettes. Their conclusions regarding false advertising of tobacco indicates
that the love of money, regardless of the cost in human
suffering and lives, verifies the Lord's warning about
conspiring men.

30

In view of the publicized health hazards a strange although
completely explicable transformation has occurred in the filter
cigarette since its introduction, Many smokers apparently found
the filters to be less satisfying (as in the case of Kents) than their
old regular cigarettes. They tried different brands, presumably in
search of a filter cigarette which not only afforded health
protection but also (as one brand advertised) "tastes good like a
cigarette should."

The cigarette manufacturers obliged—at least with respect to
taste. Unfortunately, the much advertised health protection—
that is, less nicotine and tar—was an unpublicized casualty. The
filter cigarette smoker is, in most cases, getting as much or more
nicotine and tar from the filter than he would get from the
regular cigarette the advertisers have persuaded him to
abandon—for his health's sake. ("False and Misleading
Advertising," *Twentieth Report by the Committee on Government
Operations*, United States Government Printing Office, 1958, p.
15.)

The committee expressed concern over the lack of
cooperation from the tobacco companies:

Despite repeated private and even public invitations to
appear before the subcommittee, the tobacco industry refused all
such invitations. In one instance the invitation was accepted only
to be declined later because of a "previous engagement," when it
was learned no other tobacco company official would appear.

During a period fraught with public concern over grave
health implications of cigarette smoking, business responsibility
and even decency would apparently dictate that the American
public is entitled to an accounting from the cigarette
manufacturers. It is indeed most reprehensible that the tobacco
industry should so shirk its vast responsibilities to the consumer
and apparently conspire to boycott the hearings of the
congressional committee. (Ibid., p. 23.)

Although some of the committee's findings concerned
the Federal Trade Commission's failure to approach with
vigor and diligence the problem of false and misleading ad-

vertising, the first two of the four conclusions are pertinent to us:

1. The cigarette manufacturers have deceived the American public through their advertising of filter-tip cigarettes.

Ironically, while denying the alleged health hazards of cigarette smoking, the cigarette industry has, in its advertising, made these charges appear true.

Without specifically claiming that the filter tip removes the agents alleged to contribute to heart disease or lung cancer, the advertising has emphasized such claims as "clean smoking," "snowy white," "pure," "miracle tip," "20,000 filter traps," "gives you more of what you changed to a filter for," and other phrases implying health protection, when actually most filter cigarettes produce as much or more nicotine and tar as cigarettes without filters.

2. The effectiveness of this deceptive advertising is evidenced by the rise in filter-cigarette sales from 1.4 percent of total cigarette sales in 1952 to 40 percent in 1957. The American public have paid premium prices of 2 to 6 cents per pack for filter cigarettes for "protection" they did not receive. (Ibid., pp. 24-25.)

Millions of dollars are spent yearly in advertising cigarettes, though in recent years legislation has taken advertisements for them off radio and television. There is, however, a continuing effort by conspiring men to foster this harmful product among the public, as the Lord warned.

President David O. McKay spoke in a general conference priesthood session against the methods employed by the tobacco industry when he outlined the progressive advertising used to induce women to use cigarettes:

"Evils and designs which do and will exist in the hearts of conspiring men. . . ." The purport of that impressed me in the twenties, and the thirties of this century. I just ask you men tonight to recall the methods employed by certain tobacco interests to induce women to smoke cigarettes.

You remember how insidiously they launched their plan. First, by saying that it would reduce weight. They had a slogan: "Take a cigarette instead of a sweet."

Later, some of us who like the theatre, noticed that they would have a young lady light the gentleman's cigarette.

31

Following this a woman's hand would be shown on billboards lighting or taking a cigarette. A year or two passed and soon they were brazen enough to show the lady on the screen or on the billboard smoking the cigarette.

I find here a clipping which I set aside in the early thirties, which corroborates this idea. This is 1931:

"It is well known that the cigarette manufacturers are after the young women and girls, now. They say there are twenty-five million of these in the United States, and if they can popularize smoking among them, they will be able to increase their sales from three billion, six hundred million dollars annually to six billion dollars. This is their claim and their aim." . . .

I may be wrong, but I thought I saw an indication recently that *conspiring* men now have evil designs upon our youth. Keep your eyes and ears open, to observe if they are not taking the same steps now to get our young men as they did to entice women to use that vile weed. You know that:

"Sin is a monster of such hideous mien,
As to be hated needs but to be seen,
But seen too oft, familiar with its face,
We first endure, then pity, then embrace."

(*Conference Report*, October 1949, pp. 185-87.)

Some years ago testimonies of the advantages of smoking cigarettes, the pleasures derived therefrom, and the claim that they are not harmful were solicited from professional persons in the arts and sports. Among these was Gene Tunney, former world heavyweight boxing champion, who gave this testimony:

I've always opposed the pernicious, advertising that extolls the "benefits" of tobacco-using. While I was training for my second fight with Jack Dempsey I was offered fifteen thousand dollars to endorse a certain brand of cigarettes. I didn't want to be rude, so, in declining, I merely said I didn't smoke. Next day the advertising man came back with another offer: twelve thousand dollars if I would let my picture be used with the statement that "Stinkies must be good, because all my friends smoke them." That compelled me to say what I thought—that cigarettes were a foul pestilence, and that advertising which promoted their use was a national menace.

I am here reminded of the Metropolitan Opera tenor whose picture blazoned on billboards with this joyful declamation— "Gaspies Do Not Hurt My Throat." When asked about it, he laughed and replied: "It is true Gaspies never hurt my throat—I don't smoke."

Such misleading advertising I cannot rap too hard. It is dangerous, particularly to our thirty-five million young people. To contract the tobacco habit when the growth factors of the body are exerting themselves to their maximum is to handicap oneself physically and mentally for life. (Gene Tunney, "Nicotine Knockout, or the Slow Count," *Improvement Era*, January 1942, p. 53.)

33

The Word of Wisdom also warns Latter-day Saints against the use of hot drinks: ". . . hot drinks are not for the body or belly. . . ." (D&C 89:9.) The term "hot drinks" in this revelation has been interpreted as tea and coffee, drinks commonly used when the revelation was received. (Brigham Young, *Journal of Discourses*, 13:277.)

Propaganda may be good or bad, depending upon the message being promoted. "Hot drinks" industries, especially in the United States, where about one-half of the world's coffee supply is consumed, employ propaganda methods that are designed to change people's attitudes toward their product. A motivational research agency provided the coffee industry with some recommendations determined from in-depth interviews with coffee drinkers. Their aim was to discover feelings of sin and punishment associated with the coffee-drinking habit. Three principal facts were learned from coffee drinkers that indicated the industry needed to change the image of coffee from a sinful and escapist beverage to a beneficial and life-accepting one: (1) Coffee was considered to be a drug-provoking addiction; (2) it was considered to be a dangerous drink that overstimulated the heart and other organs; and (3) it was believed to contribute to laziness.

To change a sinful image to one of morality was a large task, but the researchers felt that this transformation could be encouraged by dramatizing to the public that since coffee is a natural product, it is universally acceptable; furthermore, it helps the drinker gain independence and self-control, and children could be initiated into using coffee if it were promoted as a symbol of growing maturity. This latter suggestion could be achieved by citing some parents' success and by the use of good-humored approaches as part of the growing-up process. (Neil H. Borden and Marvin V. Marshall, *Advertising Management*, Irwin Publications, revised edition, 1959, p. 606.)

5

Wine or Strong Drink
Is Not Good

In 1942 the First Presidency of the Church issued the following message:

Drink brings cruelty into the home; it walks arm in arm with poverty; its companions are disease and plague; it puts chastity to flight; it knows neither honesty nor fair dealing; it is a total stranger to truth; it drowns conscience; it is the bodyguard of evil; it curses all who touch it.

Drink has brought more woe and misery, broken more hearts, wrecked more homes, committed more crimes, filled more coffins, than all the wars the world has suffered. (*Conference Report,* October 1942, p. 8.)

When one seriously considers this inspired statement, he wonders why this vicious enemy of mankind has not been outlawed. Yet, advertising continues to paint a beautiful picture, leaving out the sordid conditions that result from improper use of alcohol. As one writer expressed it:

No pictured man or woman drinker is ever disheveled, or silly in appearance! No boisterous gayety *en évidence!* No stagger— no, not even any swagger! Poised, masterful men; beautifully gowned, well-behaved women. No bar—no brass rail! No dim lights hesitantly peeking into dark booths. No unseemly coarseness in the relations of men and women in high-priced lounges or low-priced taverns. No such pictures! No fights; no brawls; no murders! The men who create the ads seem to know nothing of such awkward situations.

Sidney J. Harris, in his Chicago *Daily News* column, wrote a few months ago:

"I used to think of whiskey making as a simple affair. But the inspired boys who write the whiskey ads know better. Every whiskey on the market is made by a separate, special and secret blend guaranteed to afford the most exquisite delight to the man of distinction. I have learned much from reading whiskey ads.

"For instance," continues Mr. Harris, "nobody can get really stinking drunk drinking the stuff. No, it merely heightens your enjoyment of life, or strengthens the bond of good fellowship. Some distillers insinuate that their whiskey is practically all the nourishment you need, and any day I am expecting their researchers to discover some new vitamin in whiskey that will make it essential for infants. And isn't it funny that the man with the whiskey glass has the stamp of success upon him? Nobody ever gets 'potted' or beats up bartenders or fellow-drinkers, or falls down elevator shafts, or makes passes at other men's wives, or runs over kids in the streets." (Pickett, *Some Notes on the Alcohol Problem*, pp. 122-23.)

36

Some people have attempted to justify their own use of intoxicating drink on the basis of some accounts in the Bible. No attempt will be made here to present all the known facts regarding the use of wine in the Bible. Probably the best known of these accounts are the making of wine by Jesus at the wedding in Cana (John 2:1-11) and the passage from Paul: "Drink . . . a little wine for thy stomach's sake. . . ." (1 Timothy 5:23.)

One should be aware of the condemnatory statements regarding intoxicating liquors, such as: "Wine is a mocker, strong drink is raging; and whosoever is deceived thereby is not wise." (Proverbs 20:1.) "Envyings, murders, drunkenness, revellings, and such like: of the which I tell you before, as I have also told you in time past, that they which do such things shall not inherit the kingdom of God." (Galatians 5:21.) "Cease drunkenness; and let your words tend to edifying one another." (D&C 136:24.)

In summarizing some of the information about wine in the Bible, Dr. Joseph P. Free contends that the strong drink of the Bible meant light beverages, since wine was made differently then than it is today. A high concentration of alcohol is obtained by methods unknown in those days. (*Archaeology and Bible History*, Wheaton, Illinois: Scripture Press Book Division, 1956, rev., p. 352.) One Hebrew word, *tirosh*, often used in the Bible, means "new wine" or grape juice. Another word used for wine in the Old Testament, *yayin*, means fermented wine, but when examined in its various uses it does not support the use of wine. (Ibid., pp. 352-53.)

With reference to the wine served at the marriage in Cana, Dr. Free believes that this was the grape-juice variety. The reference to "good wine" (John 2:10) does not necessarily mean high alcoholic content, for wine made by Jesus would be nothing other than good. (Ibid., pp. 354-55.)

The apostle Paul's counsel that wine is good for the stomach does not support the use of alcoholic wine. The wine mentioned could mean either wine or grape juice, and the use of an alcoholic beverage in a day when medicines were few and wine was weak is understandable. (Ibid., p. 354.) This practice was in vogue in the pioneer period of the United States.

There are two major reasons why people drink: (1) the desire to conform to a social custom, and (2) the search for relaxation and release of tension. Externally, people are induced to drink because the liquor industry is in business to make money.

Social pressure or custom, that which society does as opposed to what it thinks it does or tells itself it ought to do, looms high in accounting for the great amount of drinking in the United States. Historically, many centuries ago man learned the effects of alcohol in alleviating pain, minimizing anxiety, and assuaging sorrow. Today, most of the liquor consumed is done in company with others, in the belief that this is the way to bring life and enjoyment to conversation.

Dr. Marvin A. Block, who has served as vice-president of the American Medical Society of Alcoholism and the Committee on Alcoholism and Drug Dependence of the American Medical Association, a renowned lecturer and author of several books and articles on all aspects of alcoholism, has written the following:

> Seventy-one percent of our adult population drink. Seventy-nine percent of our men and sixty-three percent of our women drink. Seventy-nine percent of the age group between twenty-one and twenty-nine drink; of the group between thirty and forty-nine, seventy-six percent drink; and persons aged fifty and over, sixty-one percent drink.
> Because of its social acceptance, alcohol is rarely thought of as a drug. But a drug it is, in scientific fact. It belongs in the category of anesthetics and embodies the same risks of dangerous consequences, when abused, as do all other drugs. . . .

Ours is a drug-oriented society—largely because of alcohol. . . .

In smaller doses, alcohol acts as a sedative. By its action on the brain, it reduces awareness of pain and discomfort, allays fears, and calms anxieties and modifies perception. If more of the drug is consumed, its anesthetic impacts are registered, with deep sleep and unconsciousness the eventual consequence. If intake is continued over an extended period, complete paralysis of the respiratory and circulatory centers occurs; and, if persisted in long enough, death will be the ultimate result. . . .

. . . it cannot be regarded as a true food, since it contains neither fats, carbohydrates nor proteins. Neither does it contain minerals or vitamins, other materials equally necessary for building body tissue. . . .

The alcoholic beverages used by modern man are many and varied—in appearance, taste and strength, but not in drug effect. What is frequently forgotten or ignored is that they have a common denominator, an unvarying organic chemical substance that, regardless of the vehicle or the concentration in which it is present, has precisely the same drug action. . . .

Alcohol itself intoxicates. And this it will unfailingly do, in proportion to the amount ingested, whether in limited volumes of distilled spirits, larger volumes of wine, or still larger volumes of beer or ale. (*Alcohol, Man and Science,* a pamphlet by Marvin A. Block, pp. 10-11, 2-4.)

The degree of alcohol's injurious effects depends upon the degree of alcoholic concentration in the blood. The more alcohol consumed, the greater is the injury. "Alcohol affects practically the entire human mechanism: a man's tissues, his organs, his mind." (Ibid., p. 5.) When taken excessively, it produces many ill effects. The liver is particularly vulnerable, because it is there that most of the alcohol is metabolized. Cirrhosis occurs in excessive drinkers eight times as frequently as among those who drink in moderation or not at all. (Ibid., p. 6.)

Dr. Richard A. Call, medical director of the Utah Valley Hospital in Provo, Utah, in an unpublished speech titled "Tissue Damage from Alcohol," says about the liver and alcohol:

The first change is infiltration of fat within the liver cells, thus disturbing the usual liver function. Degeneration and death of cells then occurs with replacement by dense scar tissue. These

are long-term changes and may be reversible if drinking is
stopped in sufficient time. However, if the drinking persists, more
and more functional liver tissue is destroyed, thus accentuating
and compounding the damage within the organ. Abnormal liver
function follows, with eventual death of the patient. Clinically,
the patient may waste away due to the inadequate and improper
utilization of food, particularly the inadequate protein
metabolism which disturbs the osmotic equilibrium. Thus the
liquid fraction of the blood then leaks into the tissue, causing
swelling of the extremities and fluid develops within the
abdomen, chest cavities, and around the heart. Cirrhosis of the
liver is found in 2 to 3 percent of all autopsies and is most
frequent between the ages of 45 and 64 years. It ranks fourth in
cause of death in the United States behind heart disease,
cancer, and stroke.

39

Inasmuch as alcohol does not require digestion, it is
absorbed into the bloodstream directly through the walls of
the stomach; therefore, in one way or another it affects
every tissue and organ except the bones.

Dr. Call discusses the effects of alcohol within the gastrointestinal tract:

The most lethal effects are those within the gastrointestinal
tract. Ingestion of the high percentage alcohols within the 40 to
50 percent range without dilution or without use of mixer
ofttimes results in a severe inflammation of the mucus
membranes lining the mouth, esophagus, stomach and intestine.
The lesion in the stomach is called acute alcoholic gastritis and is
due to the direct effect of the concentrated alcohol upon these
cells. They become intensely inflamed and in many cases swollen.
This inflammatory or irritating effect may become increasingly
severe until these membranes are permanently damaged.

Regarding cancer and alcohol, Dr. Call says: "Cancer
of the mouth and esophagus occurs more frequently among
drinkers." He concludes also that hemorrhagic pancreatitis
is often associated with alcoholism. Hemorrhage into the
pancreas may result in the death of cells with liberation of
enzymes that may digest body tissues; excavating wounds
of the anterior abdominal wall may follow. (Ibid.)

In discussing the conspicuous effects of alcohol upon
the cells of the nervous system, Dr. Call says:

It has been shown by Armed Forces scientists that swelling of the brain and oxygen lack occurs during acute alcoholic intoxication in addition to the direct toxic effect upon the brain cells with interference of cell respiration and metabolism. Periodic intoxication leads to a gradual cumulative loss of cells with possible resultant disturbed judgment, etc.

40

Acute alcoholic episodes may result in death when the concentration of alcohol in the blood reaches the vicinity of 0.4 mg. percent or 10 to 12 one-ounce highballs. Evidence is clear that in strong concentrations, alcohol will destroy nerve cells and result in death. This may be either from nerve cell destruction and/or marked depression of the vital centers within the central nervous system. For example, if the respiratory center or the cardiac center within the brain is depressed sufficiently, death may ensue from suffocation or heart standstill. Alcohol definitely results in slower respirations and more feeble respiratory efforts due to the toxic action on these centers within the brain.

Dr. Block also describes the effects of alcohol on the central nervous system:

Since alcohol is a central nervous system depressant, all brain functions are affected—including that which controls behavior. By depressing those centers which normally exercise the restraint responsible for a person's proper behavior, inhibitions are released and his conduct is radically changed. There is an illusion of stimulation at first, of increased aggressiveness and reckless enterprise; talk grows louder and more flamboyant; laughter becomes more raucous and may become hysterical; the person becomes less careful of what he says and does. His performance breaks into a new and stepped-up tempo that for a time at least may be maintained. This is perfectly true. But it isn't because of more gas in his carburetor, but because alcohol has reached his brain and lowered his natural controls. He is merely less inhibited and so gives freer rein to his impulses. And, as the quick energy he at first derived from alcohol is used up, he will gradually lose his artificial buoyancy and before long his activity will drop below what is normal for him. In an effort to prolong his freedom from inhibition, the uncontrolled drinker will consume more and more alcohol. Such continued ingestion will eventually depress all brain centers to the point where all activity will cease. (*Alcohol, Man and Science,* p. 5.)

President Heber J. Grant once said: "The Lord says it is not good, and all the legislatures and all the congresses and all the senators and all the officers in the kingdoms of the world can say otherwise, but that will not change the word of the Creator of heaven and earth." (*Conference Report,* April 1933, p. 7.)

Furthermore, he declared:

> But I am very grateful indeed that the repeal of the Eighteenth Amendment will not make any difference to any true Latter-day Saint. No Latter-day Saint will patronize those things when the Lord has told us it is His will that we let them alone. If our people are going to take license to follow after the things of the world and the people of the world, and do those things that the gospel of Jesus Christ teaches them not to do, they are not living up to their religion. So, really, the repeal of the Eighteenth Amendment will make no difference whatever to a true Latter-day Saint. (*Gospel Standards,* pp. 145-46.)

41

The Lord's word to this generation on the subject of alcohol and the interpretation of that word were given by David O. McKay while he was a member of the Council of the Twelve:

> The particular sentence that I wish to call attention to is this: "Inasmuch as any man drinketh wine or strong drink * * * behold *it is not good,* neither meet in the sight of your Father." That is the word of God to the people of this generation. It stands with just as much force as the words of the Savior, "If any man will do His will, he shall know of the doctrine, whether it be of God or whether I speak of myself." [John 7:17] . . . Just so strong, just so eternal stands this truth expressed seventy-eight years ago, the 27th day of last February, "Strong drink is not good for man." Yet those seventy-eight years have passed, and during that time this doctrine has been preached every week, if not every day, in some congregation of Israel, and still we find in our midst a few who say, by their acts, It is good for man. I am glad when I study this passage, to find that the Lord did not say, "Strong drink to *excess* is not good;" nor "Drunkenness is not good." Suppose He had weakened that expression by modifying it and saying, "Strong drink in excess, or when taken in large quantities, is not good," how soon we should have justified ourselves that a little drink is good. But like other eternal truths it stands unqualified; *strong drink is not good.* I have met men, particularly during the agitation that is now manifested against the liquor evil, who have said: "I do not want to be deprived of the privilege of taking a little, if I want it. When I think it is going to do me good, I want to take it." Others, I rather think, would say that the Church is a little too strict in regard to the word of wisdom: "A little beer," they say, "does not hurt any one; a little wine is not

injurious." Well, it is sufficient for me to know that God has said, "Wine, strong drink, is not good for man;" and I wish that all Israel would accept that divine statement, and prove in their lives to the whole world that they accept this as a revelation from God. (*Conference Report,* April 1911, p. 62.)

42

Much of the material already discussed is concerned with the excessive or near-excessive drinker, but what of the so-called moderate drinker? Who is an excessive drinker, and who is a moderate drinker? Dr. L. Weston Oaks gives the following thought on this question:

> Actually *moderate drinking* is a purely relative and indefinite term that no authority has, as yet, offered a clear definition of. Its far boundary appears to be drunkenness; but the dividing line between the two is a wide band fading imperceptibly into each. (*The Word of Wisdom and You,* p. 126.)

Dr. Charles H. Durfee believes that a relevant criterion might be the effect of the individual's drinking on his life. Alcohol becomes a problem to a person if his drinking affects his family life, his work, or his social relations. (Dean Pickett, *Some Notes on the Alcohol Problem,* p. 53.)

The use of alcoholic beverages even in small amounts affects a person to some degree. As stated by the Widtsoes: ". . . a man under the influence of even small doses of alcoholic liquor becomes an altered individual—always altered for the worse." (*The Word of Wisdom, A Modern Interpretation,* rev. ed., p. 37.)

No one knows what the first drink may lead to. The craving for alcohol is an unknown in individual cases and must be triggered when the use of it begins. Dr. Block gives this informative information about the movement from moderation to alcoholism:

> It should be remembered that no sharp line of demarcation separates the social drinker from the alcoholic. Rather, there is a hazy area across which the drinker may float from one classification into the other. Only the expert, by means of close interrogation and detailed history taking, can detect significant changes in drinking patterns.
> It is extremely important that the fact be recognized that any adverse result consistent with drinking may be the forerunner of

alcohol problems. Whether these adverse effects be psychological
or physiological is of little importance so long as they are adverse.
Alcohol then can be assumed to be a detrimental agent in direct
proportion to the adverse effects it demonstrates. . . .

Even so, if the observable adverse effects of even moderate
drinking are consistent, the drinker must be strongly warned
against continuing the risk of greater involvement. For the
dangers become more serious the longer they are denied or
ignored. Disaster becomes even more possible and avoidance of it
even more arduous. (*Alcohol, Man and Science*, p. 5.)

Some further adverse effects of use of alcoholic
beverages might be mentioned. The economic impact of
alcohol in the United States is tremendous. Billions of
dollars are lost to industry each year in absenteeism, lower
productivity, accidents and general inefficiency. Care of alcoholics in institutions represents a very large sum, which
is paid by taxpayers. Nine million Americans—or almost
ten percent of the nation's work force—are alcoholics.
They and their problems affect the lives of another forty
million people, including many children.

The loss in human life is staggering. About one-half of
all traffic injuries and deaths (some 50,000 killed and
800,000 injured each year) are considered to be
attributable to drinking. This problem is aggravated by
public acceptance of drinking drivers. In fact, 50 percent of
all violent deaths—accidents, suicides, and homicides—
have an alcohol factor. Actuarial tables grant the alcoholic
a life expectancy of twelve years less than that of the non-
alcoholic.

As important as are the adverse physical and economic
consequences of drinking, of far greater magnitude is the
impairment of religious life. When one considers the short
period of earth life and the revealed purpose of life—to
prepare for the blessings of eternity—the loss of faith in
Christ as man's Atoner and Redeemer is a high price to
pay for indulgence that cannot be measured in money or
life. Here are some of the consequences of using alcoholic
beverages, even moderately.

With the loss of judgment and lowering of behavioral
standards, drinking contributes to criminal acts. It is a fact

that liquor is the greatest single source of crime. (Dobyns, *The Amazing Story of Repeal,* p. 428.)

From the standpoint of religious life, the most devastating behavior to decrease faith and spirituality is sexual immorality. Alcohol desensitizes conscience and lowers normal inhibitions. Under the influence of intoxicating beverages, even in moderate amounts, people yield to sexual temptations to which they would not otherwise succumb.

Spiritual development is retarded, if not stopped, when one indulges in liquor. An indictment against liquor was made by President David O. McKay:

> The world today perhaps as never before needs more spirituality. Booze and depravity mingle together harmoniously, but booze and spirituality, never. . . .
> No one will contend that intoxicating liquors contribute spirituality either to the individual or to the nation. Nearly everyone concedes that intoxicants develop the baser, not the finer, things of life. (*Gospel Ideals,* p. 373.)

Dr. Morris E. Chafetz, director of the National Institute on Alcohol Abuse and Alcoholism, a recently established federal agency, reports an alarming increase in drunkenness among teenagers: "Studies show that, in the last ten years, arrests of girls eighteen and younger intoxicated by liquor have more than tripled. During the same period, arrests of boys in the same age group have more than doubled." ("The Tippling American: On the Rocks," *PTA Magazine,* May 1973, p. 17.) According to Dr. Chafetz, about 60 percent of American youths say they have drunk or tasted alcoholic beverages, and about one-third drink with some regularity. As few as 20 percent and as many as 80 percent in some communities say they have used alcohol. The first taste of alcohol often occurs before the age of thirteen, and sometimes this occurs in the home. The urge to experiment is the usual cause for the first drink, beer being the most popular choice. Some young people claim that they use alcohol in order to rebel against parents, while others take license in drinking because of the use of alcohol in the home.

Parents are the models who set behavior patterns for youth, and many American youth see their parents using such drugs as tranquilizers, pain-killers, sleep-inducers, and alcohol; consequently, Dr. Chafetz observes, "In this kind of environment, it would be the unusual youth who wouldn't at least experiment with alcohol." (Ibid., p. 17.)

45

In order to consume the wine production of the 1930s, the French government gave wine to school children, claiming it to be a digestive aid. This polluted the man-power pool and affected the French army. Permissiveness of parents regarding their children and use of alcoholic beverages causes innumerable children as young as six years of age to become addicted. (*Alcohol: Who Is Allergic?*, 1966 annual report of Eversharp, Inc., p. 17.)

Latter-day Saint youths should be those who have learned from their parents' knees early in life that obedience to the Word of Wisdom is a most important part of gospel practice that will pay high dividends throughout life. Latter-day Saint parents should never lead their children to break God's commandments, and they should live exemplary lives themselves, knowing that a high degree of spirituality is achieved by keeping one's body clean and pure. President N. Eldon Tanner of the First Presidency related this story, one that would never happen to a faithful Latter-day Saint parent:

> I would like to refer to a story that I have often mentioned about the father who was called to the scene of a car accident in which his young daughter was killed. The group had been drinking, and the father in his anguish exclaimed: "I'll kill the man who provided this whiskey!" On returning home he found a note in his daughter's own handwriting in his liquor cabinet. It read: "Dad, I hope you don't mind our taking your whiskey tonight." (*The Improvement Era*, August 1968, p. 6.)

To faithful Latter-day Saints the First Presidency in 1942 gave their blessing—and their admonition to other members of the Church:

> Therefore, we thank the faithful Saints for their observance of the Word of Wisdom, for their putting aside of drink. The Lord is pleased with you. You have been a bulwark of strength to

this people and to the world. Your influence has been for righteousness. The Lord will not forget your good works when you stand before Him in judgment. He has blessed and will continue to bless you with the blessings He promised to those who obey this divine law of health. We invoke the mercies of the Lord upon you that you may continue strong in spirit, to cast off temptation and continue teachers to the youth of Zion by word and deed.

46

But so great is the curse of drink that we should not be held guiltless did we not call upon all offending Saints to forsake it and banish it from their lives forever. (*Conference Report,* October 1942, p. 8.)

6

Tobacco...
Is Not Good for Man

Have you ever really considered what a cigaret means to a
Latter-day Saint? You who smoke now, do not make the mistake
of supposing that the Church is against you, because it is not. It
only desires your welfare, and it hopes and prays for the day
when you will declare your independence from the slavery of
nicotine. And you who do not smoke, before you take that first
cigaret ask yourself, "Will it help me or hurt me?" (Mark E.
Petersen, *Conference Report*, April 1948, p. 156.)

"Will it help me or hurt me?" may be answered cate-
gorically: tobacco will *not* help one. In fact, it will destroy a
Latter-day Saint's spiritual life and cause him physical
harm.

We have seen that for some decades, in their quest for
wealth and without regard for the welfare of their
fellowmen, men have promoted vigorously the sale of
products inimical to health. Among these harmful
products is tobacco. Ever since scientific information revealing the dangerous effects of cigarette smoking has been
widely disseminated, tobacco companies have fought
against the truth and propagandized the public with im-
mense sums of money.

An example of these evil designs was exposed in the
"Medical Bulletin on Tobacco [for physicians]," published
in April 1968 by the American Public Health Association,
American Heart Association, American Cancer Society,
and National Tuberculosis Association. *True* magazine had
published an article entitled "To Smoke or Not to
Smoke—That Is *Still* the Question," which was sent to
physicians, lawyers, schoolteachers, and other opinion
leaders, claiming that "there is absolutely no proof that
smoking causes human cancer." Two mailings of this
article were made, one for tobacco company stockholders
and the other for opinion leaders. The latter mailing did
not give any reference to the cigarette industry or its

known publicity agents. This massive propaganda effort by the tobacco industry was commented upon by the American Cancer Society in answering the question, "Why is this being given this handsome layout, rich paper, and massive distribution to opinion leaders?"

48

> Perhaps because it wraps up in lively journalese the tobacco industry's long-time effort to merchandise doubt, to give cigarette smokers the impression that a major scientific controversy rages over whether cigarettes are harmful, that "only statistics" indict cigarette smoking as an extraordinarily dangerous habit. . . .
>
> A host of health organizations (governmental and voluntary, here and abroad) have considered the evidence, in many cases have worked to produce the evidence through investigation, and are convinced that the cigarette is a distinct menace to health and life itself. The American Medical Association itself has indicted cigarette smoking as "a serious health hazard." ("The Medical Bulletin," pp. 1-2.)

Is the evidence only "statistical," as alleged? The "Medical Bulletin" answers:

> In 1960, the American Cancer Society issued a statement in which it said: ". . . clinical, epidemiological [population group], experimental, chemical, and pathological evidence presented by many studies . . . indicates beyond reasonable doubt that cigarette smoking is the major cause of the unprecedented increase in lung cancer."
>
> Over the intervening years, the evidence—of all types—has grown both in magnitude and in conviction. (Ibid., p. 2.)

What are some of the discoveries of this research? Again, this answer is given:

> Despite the propaganda of the cigarette industry, cigarette smoking has been established as most hazardous.
>
> Every regular cigarette smoker is injured though not in the same degree. Cigarette smoking kills some, makes others lung cripples, gives still others far more than their share of illness and loss of work days. Cigarette smoking is not a gamble; all regular cigarette smokers studied at autopsy show the effects. (Ibid., p. 3.)

The public has been lulled for a long time with the false idea that cigarette smoking is harmless or that the harmful results of smoking are a gamble and far in the future, so that a false sense of security has developed.

In the following excerpt from a general conference sermon, President N. Eldon Tanner of the First Presidency exposes the futility of such a belief:

Dr. William H. Stewart has said the so-called "next-guy theory"—that it can happen to someone else but not to me—is the psychology that is preventing anti-cigarette campaigns from making more headway. The fallacy of this kind of reasoning is illustrated in the story of a Honolulu reporter, who said, "It just can't happen to me; I'm safe." But this Hawaiian newsman, Mark Waters, spoke from the grave to readers of the Honolulu *Star Bulletin.* Waters died of lung cancer at the age of 56 on February 1, the day the *Star Bulletin* ran his last story. It was a by-line account of a 42-year rendezvous with his killer.

The story was written in the hospital five days before his death. Waters read proof on the story and made final corrections the day before he succumbed, observing that it might help someone else.

Waters told how he started smoking at 14, stealing cigarettes from his father's pack, and how he continued at the rate of two packs a day, even after suffering a stroke and contracting bronchitis. Doctors discovered cancer in his left lung. A lobe was removed. Waters gained 10 pounds after the September operation and felt fine. Four months later pain returned. The doctor removed fluid from his chest cavity but had to tell him that he had little time to live.

"Not a soul I've preached to has stopped smoking," he wrote from his hospital bed, "not a single, solitary soul.

"It's one of those things. You always think, it'll happen to others, but never to me. When you get lung cancer, God help you."

Like the rest of his story, Waters' conclusion was terse.

"I'm short of breath. I can't take five steps without having to sit.

"The cancer has gone to my liver and I don't know where else.

"I don't have a ghost of a chance.

"It's too late for me.

"It may not be for you." (*Conference Report*, April 1966, p. 104.)

Some people who have smoked for a long period of time say, "I have smoked for so long, it won't do any good to stop, because the damage has been done."

The Latter-day Saint knows that the blessings received

from observing *all* provisions of the Word of Wisdom extend far beyond physical health benefits. The spiritual blessings of the eternities await those who observe the Lord's commandments.

Recent studies released by the U.S. Department of Health, Education, and Welfare indicate that the risk of death from coronary heart disease is decreased when cigarette smokers quit the habit. (*The Health Consequences of Smoking*, a Report to the Surgeon General, 1971, p. 8.)

The following summary of findings pertains to lung cancer:

> These studies [epidemiological, experimental, and pathological] reveal that the risk of developing lung cancer increases with the number of cigarettes smoked per day, the duration of smoking, and earlier initiation, and diminishes with cessation of smoking. (Ibid., p. 11.)

In a report issued in 1967, the following detailed information on this subject was given:

> In general, the greater the number of cigarettes smoked daily the higher the death rate. For men who smoke fewer than 10 cigarettes a day, according to the seven prospective studies, the death rate from all causes is about 40 percent higher than for nonsmokers. For those who smoke from 10 to 19 cigarettes a day, it is about 70 percent higher than for nonsmokers; for those who smoke 20 to 39 a day, 90 percent higher; and for those who smoke 40 or more, it is 120 percent higher.
>
> Cigarette smokers who stopped smoking before enrolling in the seven studies have a death rate about 40 percent higher than nonsmokers, as against 70 percent higher for current cigarette smokers. Men who began smoking before age 20 have a substantially higher death rate than those who began after age 25. Compared with nonsmokers, the mortality risk of cigarette smokers, after adjustments for differences in age, increases with duration of smoking (number of years), and is higher in those who stopped after age 55 than for those who stopped at an earlier age.
>
> In two studies which recorded the degree of inhalation, the mortality ratio for a given amount of smoking was greater for inhalers than for noninhalers. (*The Health Consequences of Smoking*, A Public Health Service Review, 1967, p. 7.)

The 1971 Surgeon General's report suggested that

"cigarette smoking initiates a disease process by producing progressive irreversible damage. In this case, the total effect would be approximately proportional to the total accumulated dosage experienced over the years." (*Op. cit.*, p. 4.) The more cigarettes one smokes over a long period of time, the greater is the risk of illness and death. Dr. Alton Ochsner, the "grand old man of the antismoking crusade," related to the Brigham Young University student body the experience of Dr. Everetts Graham, his teacher and professor of surgery at Washington University in St. Louis, who used to chide him about the relationship of smoking and cancer.

He himself was a heavy smoker. He didn't think there was a causal relationship. I must admit from the beginning my reasons for it were pretty nebulous. They were based upon two facts. One, at that time I had never seen a patient with cancer of the lung who had not been a heavy smoker, and the other was that there was a parallelism between consumption of cigarettes and the incidence of cancer of the lung. Dr. Graham used to say, "Yes, there is a parallelism between the consumption of cigarettes and the incidence of cancer of the lung, but there is also a parallelism between the incidence of cancer of the lung and the sale of nylon stockings," which there was about fifteen years ago. Dr. Graham, however, subsequently became convinced . . . that there was a causal relationship, and stopped. He died of cancer of the lung. The saddest letter I ever got in my life I got from Everetts Graham three weeks before he died. He said, "I just want to let you know, and I know of your interest, that they've just found that I've got cancer in both of my lungs. You know, I stopped smoking four years ago, but too much damage had been done." We lost a great man when we lost Everetts Graham. He died of the disease which he did so much to elucidate. (*Tobacco and Cancer of the Lung*, forum assembly address at Brigham Young University, May 20, 1959.)

In considering the potential health benefits of giving up smoking, the same study determined that there were degrees ranging from substantial benefits to no benefits. In the former case, the probability of myocardial damage is increased with each cigarette smoked, but if smoking is stopped, the probability of damage becomes normal. Since cirrhosis of the liver is associated with the drinking of alcoholic beverages, and heavy consumers of these beverages are nearly always smokers, to stop smoking would not give any direct benefit. (*The Health Consequences of Smoking,* 1971, pp. 4-5.)

52

Not long after the introduction of tobacco into Spain and England in the early part of the sixteenth century, people began to ask whether or not tobacco was good for one's health. As its production and use increased, especially the smoking of cigarettes, the controversy intensified.

The modern period of investigation of smoking and health began around 1900, and vital statistics noted an increase in cancer of the lung. Studies began to center on the relationship of smoking and other uses of tobacco to cancer of the lung and other organs as well as other diseases of the organs of the body. In 1930 definite trends in mortality and the incidence of disease due to tobacco were becoming evident. Many experiments were made involving lower animals, exposing them to smoke and tars, gases, and various constituents in tobacco and tobacco smoke. Between 1939 and 1969 twenty-nine studies were conducted dealing with data from the personal histories and medical and mortality records of individuals and groups.

From "Smoking and Health, Report of the Advisory Committee to the Surgeon General of the Public Health Service, January 1964," from which the foregoing historical information was taken, the following paragraph is informative.

> During the decade 1950-1960, at various dates, statements based upon the accumulated evidence were issued by a number of organizations. These included the British Medical Research Council; the cancer societies of Denmark, Norway, Sweden, Finland, and the Netherlands; the American Cancer Society; the American Heart Association; the Joint Tuberculosis Council of Great Britain; and the Canadian National Department of Health and Welfare. The consensus, publicly declared, was that smoking is an important health hazard, particularly with respect to lung cancer and cardiovascular disease. (Page 6.)

Surgeon General Leroy E. Burney issued statements in 1957 and 1959 condemning cigarette smoking as a cause of lung cancer. Later, Surgeon General Luther L. Terry appointed a committee of experts to undertake a comprehensive review of all data on smoking and health. The report of the Surgeon General's Advisory Committee on Smoking and Health in 1964 arrived at this conclusion: "Cigarette smoking is a health hazard of sufficient importance in the United States to warrant appropriate remedial action." (*The Health Consequences of Smoking*, A Report to the Surgeon General, 1971, p. 3.)

53

The following summaries of the most recent report (1971) emphasize earlier conclusions, beginning with the 1964 Surgeon General's Report:

CORONARY HEART DISEASE [narrowing or blockage of the coronary arteries that supply blood to these heart muscles resulting in myocardial infarction or heart attack]

Data from numerous prospective and retrospective studies confirm the judgment that cigarette smoking is a significant risk factor contributing to the development of coronary heart disease, including fatal CHD [coronary heart disease] and its most severe expression, sudden and unexpected death. The risk of CHD incurred by smoking of pipes and cigars is appreciably less than that incurred by cigarette smokers. (Page 8.)

CEREBROVASCULAR DISEASE [narrowing or blockage of the arteries of the brain which may result in stroke]

Data from numerous prospective studies indicate that cigarette smoking is associated with increased mortality from cerebrovascular disease. (Page 9.)

CHRONIC OBSTRUCTIVE BRONCHOPULMONARY DISEASE [narrowing of the air tubes to the lungs, or reduction in numbers of honeycomb-like air sacs of the lung. Oxygen and carbon dioxide exchange takes place in these air sacs.]

Cigarette smoking is the most important cause of chronic obstructive bronchopulmonary disease in the United States. Cigarette smoking increases the risk of dying from pulmonary emphysema and chronic bronchitis. Cigarette smokers show an increased prevalence of respiratory symptoms, including cough, sputum production, and breathlessness, when compared with nonsmokers. . . .

Ex-cigarette smokers have lower death rates from COPD than do continuing smokers. The cessation of cigarette smoking is associated with improvement in ventilatory function and with a decrease in pulmonary symptom prevalence. (Pages 9-10.)

LUNG CANCER Evidence derived from a number of . . . studies, coupled with experimental and pathological autopsy or surgical evidence, confirms the conclusion that cigarette smoking is the *main cause* of lung cancer in men. These studies reveal that the risk of developing lung cancer increases with the number of cigarettes smoked per day, the duration of smoking, and earlier initiation, and diminishes with cessation of smoking. . . .

54

The risk of developing lung cancer among pipe and/or cigar smokers is higher than for nonsmokers but significantly lower than for cigarette smokers. . . .

Ex-cigarette smokers have significantly lower death rates for lung cancer than continuing smokers. (Page 11.)

CANCER OF THE LARYNX [voice box] Epidemiological, experimental, and pathological [autopsy and surgical] studies support the conclusion that cigarette smoking is a significant factor in the causation of cancer of the larynx. The risk of developing laryngeal cancer among cigarette smokers is significantly higher than among nonsmokers. The magnitude of the risk for pipe and cigar smokers is about the same order as that for cigarette smokers, or possibly slightly lower. (Page 12.)

ORAL CANCER [cancer of lips, tongue, or mouth] Studies contribute to the conclusion that smoking is a significant factor in the development of cancer of the oral cavity and that pipe smoking, alone or in conjunction with other forms of tobacco use, is related to cancer of the lip. (Page 12.)

CANCER OF THE ESOPHAGUS Epidemiological studies have demonstrated that cigarette smoking is associated with the development of cancer of the esophagus. The risk of developing esophageal cancer among pipe and/or cigar smokers is greater than for nonsmokers and/or about the same order of magnitude as for cigarette smokers, or perhaps slightly lower.

Epidemiological studies have also indicated an association between esophageal cancer and alcohol consumption and that alcohol consumption may interact with cigarette smoking. This combination of exposure is associated with especially high rates of cancer of the esophagus. (Pages 12-13.)

CANCER OF THE URINARY BLADDER AND KIDNEY Epidemiological studies have demonstrated an association of cigarette smoking with cancer of the urinary bladder among men. The association of tobacco usage and cancer of the kidney is less clear-cut. (Page 13.)

CANCER OF THE PANCREAS Epidemiological studies have suggested an association between cigarette smoking and cancer of the pancreas. The significance of the relationship is not clear at this time. (Page 13.)

PEPTIC ULCER [ulcer of the stomach or duodenum] Cigarette

smoking males have an increased prevalence of peptic ulcer
disease and a greater peptic ulcer mortality rate. These
relationships are stronger for gastric ulcer than for duodenal
ulcer. Smoking appears to reduce the effectiveness of standard
peptic ulcer treatment and to slow the rate of ulcer healing. (Page
13.)

55

Smoking mothers, on the average, have smaller babies
than do nonsmoking mothers. The incidence of premature
births is increased in smoking mothers; also, babies born to
mothers who smoke are more often stillborn or likely to die
soon after birth than are babies born to nonsmoking
mothers.

In 1965 the National Clearinghouse for Smoking and
Health was established for the continuous monitoring,
compilation, and review of the world's medical literature
that bears upon the health consequences of smoking. As a
result, the 1971 report was submitted to the Congress of
the United States as a report to the Surgeon General. Two
additional reports have subsequently been published, in
1972 and in 1973. Those reports verify earlier studies and
also give emphasis to research studies made since the last
report was published. If the reader is interested in a continuing study of the most recent information, he might obtain it from the Superintendent of Documents, U.S.
Government Printing Office, Washington, D.C. 20402, or
from his local public library.

Confirmation of earlier scientific research results and
additional subsequent findings is illustrated by the following:

Six times since 1964, the Public Health Service has issued
formal reviews of the scientific evidence which links cigarette
smoking to disease and premature death. Each successive review,
including this one, has served to confirm and strengthen the
conclusion of the 1964 Report, that cigarettes are a major cause
of death and disease. . . .

Research in smoking and health continues, as this report
shows, both in this country and abroad and under both public
and private auspices; furthermore, the range of this research is
widening as the significance of cigarette smoking as a public
health problem becomes more apparent. ("Preface," *The Health
Consequences of Smoking*, A Report of the Surgeon General, 1972.)

What about the pipe and cigar smoker? He is not free from contracting cancer, as he might suppose. Some cigarette smokers have made such a smoking change in order to free themselves from the ill effects of the cigarette. The 1973 Report to the Surgeon General carries these conclusions:

> Pipe and cigar smokers in the United States as a group experience overall mortality rates that are slightly higher than those of nonsmokers, but these rates are substantially lower than those of cigarette smokers. This appears to be due to the fact that the total exposure to smoke that a pipe or cigar smoker receives from these products is relatively low. . . . As a result, the harmful effects of cigar and pipe smoking appear to be largely limited to increased death rates from cancer at those sites which are exposed to the smoke of these products. *Mortality rates from cancer of the oral cavity, intrinsic and extrinsic larynx, pharynx, and esophagus are approximately equal in users of cigar, pipes, and cigarettes.* Inhalation is evidently not necessary to expose these sites to tobacco smoke. Although these are serious forms of cancer, they account for only about 5 percent mortality among men. [Italics added.]
>
> Evidence from countries where smokers tend to consume more cigars and inhale them to a greater degree than in the United States indicates that rates of lung cancer become elevated to levels approaching those of cigarette smokers. (Page 229.)

It has become standard practice for many coaches of athletic teams and for many athletes themselves not to smoke cigarettes. Shortness of breath and impaired performance are associated with the use of tobacco. (Alton Ochsner, *Smoking and Health*, New York: Julian Messner, Inc., 1961, p. 73.)

The 1973 Report of the Surgeon General was the first report to contain information on cigarette smoking and exercise performance. Fitness tests administered to both smokers and nonsmokers indicated that cigarette smoking impairs exercise performance, reduces the amount of oxygen received, and impairs heart and lung functioning. (*The Health Consequences of Smoking*, January 1973, p. 247.)

One study involving rest and the period after exercise of smokers indicated that the smoking of two cigarettes produces significant heart rate increases. Significantly higher and more prolonged elevations of blood pressure were shown in exercise tests preceded by smoking than in tests where the exercise was not preceded by smoking. (Ibid., p. 242.)

During the past twenty years, one-half of all the physicians in Great Britain who smoked cigarettes have stopped smoking. (Ibid., p. 240.) The number of physicians in the United States who are nonsmokers has increased during the past few years. In 1964 slightly more than one-half, or 52.2 percent, were nonsmokers; in 1966, there were 58.8 percent; in 1970 nearly two-thirds, or 63.1 percent, were reported as nonsmokers in a survey of 34,627 doctors. (*Modern Medicine*, December 28, 1970, p. 47.)

Dr. Alton Ochsner reports that a 1957 study of the smoking habits of seventy-two lung-cancer scientists showed that there were far fewer smokers among cancer specialists. (*Smoking and Your Life*, New York: Julian Messner, Inc., 1965, p. 95.)

Although it is estimated that 360,000 people die yearly in the United States from the use of tobacco, people continue to smoke. Dr. Ochsner observed that while this information is not sufficient to encourage many from discontinuing smoking, when he tells them that tobacco may result in decreased sexual activity, people suddenly take notice. ("Is Your Sex Life Going Up in Smoke?" *Today's Health*, August 1975, p. 51.) Many physicians and researchers have concluded that decreased sexual activity of men in their thirties and forties can be traced to heavy smoking. (Alton Ochsner, *Smoking and Cancer, A Doctor's Report*, New York: Julian Messner, Inc., 1954, p. 28.)

In a study of cigarette smoking among Portland, Oregon, high school students, it was learned that each successive school grade had a higher percentage of boys and girls who smoked. About 15 percent of the boys and 5 percent of the girls in the freshman class smoked regularly, while the percentage of seniors who smoked was 35 and 26 respectively.

Significantly, heavy smokers did not go out for sports; they shunned mentally demanding subjects; and there was a lack of interest in social and hobby clubs. As Dr. Ochsner observed, the deadening of the mind and body during a crucial period in life is criminal. (*Smoking and Your Life*, pp. 104-105.) This observation becomes more meaningful because the study revealed that the percentage of smokers was highest among children of families in which both parents smoked and lowest in families where neither parent smoked. Smoking parents endanger their children's health and contribute to their delinquency as much as does the bartender who sells liquor to minors. (Ibid., p. 102.)

The power to enslave is a significant factor in the evil that tobacco perpetuates. The younger one is when he becomes addicted to the smoking habit, the greater is the chance that he will be unable to shake the habit.

The father of psychoanalysis, Dr. Sigmund Freud, smoked twenty cigars a day. Because of a heart condition he was ordered by his doctor to stop smoking, which he did for several weeks; however, he then returned to his cigars, and his heart condition worsened. A second time he stopped smoking, but he started the practice again until he was back up to twenty cigars a day. He suffered from heart disease and often was unable to work. Finally he developed cancer of the jaw and had a series of thirty-three operations over a period of sixteen years. His doctors noticed that at the times he quit smoking his heart condition improved, but he would not stop completely, and his heart disease became more serious when he resumed smoking. Forty-five years of his life were sheer hell because of his heart problem and the cancer operations. (Ibid., pp. 95-96.)

Regardless of whatever pleasure is derived from smoking, the cost is too great. A Latter-day Saint youth reared in a home where neither parent uses tobacco may be spared the ill health and suffering that eventually result from cigarette use. This blessing is only one of the plus advantages that come to the obedient.

Hyrum Smith, Patriarch to the Church and brother of the Prophet Joseph, wrote:

Tobacco is a nauseous, stinking, abominable thing, and I am surprised that any human being should think of using it—for an

58

elder especially to eat, or smoke it, is a disgrace to him—he is not fit for the office; he ought first to keep the word of wisdom, and then to teach others. God will not prosper the man who uses it. (*Times and Seasons*, 3:800, 1842.)

7

Tobacco and Man
Three Powerful Messages

Much has been written about the evils of smoking and the use of tobacco in any form. Following are three powerful messages on why Latter-day Saints should observe the Word of Wisdom and particularly the admonition concerning nonuse of tobacco.

The first message, by Elder Mark E. Petersen of the Council of the Twelve, tells of the loss of spirituality that results from smoking.

The second message, by S. S. Field and reprinted with permission from the *Reader's Digest*, is an indictment of the cigarette because of the deadly poisons found in nicotine.

The third message is the personal experience of Hugh J. Mooney of Rochester, New York, who tells of the mental agony, pain, and suffering he experienced as a cigarette smoker.

Cigarettes and Spirituality
By Mark E. Petersen
of the Council of the Twelve

I wonder, young people of the Church, if you have ever seriously thought about what a cigaret means to a Latter-day Saint. It means more to us than it does to other people. I know that some of you will say that you do not see why, that you have friends in other churches who smoke, and they seem to get along all right, and their churches do not criticize them for it, and you do not see why our Church takes the attitude it does on this subject. Just remember, if you will, that the Lord has not spoken to your young friends in the other churches, nor to the heads of their churches, giving them any divine revelation directing them to abstain from these harmful things. In their churches they do not even accept the principle of modern revelation.

But with us, it is entirely different. God has spoken to us by his latter-day prophets. He has given us modern-day revelation, declaring that tobacco is not good for man. That is the word and the will of the Lord to the Latter-day Saints. Whenever we turn our backs upon that principle, to that extent we turn our backs upon the Lord.

The average young American is an individual who loves freedom, wants to be his own boss, and does not like to have other people regulate his life for him. But some of them misunderstand their independence, and in a spirit of misunderstanding say, "Well, if I want to take a smoke, that is my business. I have a perfect right to. It is a free country, isn't it?" But in submitting to the enslaving influence of nicotine, they contribute to a loss of the very freedom they talk about.

61

If you adopt the cigaret habit, it will, in large measure, determine the kind of life you are going to live, the kind of friends you will have, the kind of person you are going to marry, even the kind of children you may have. Do you regard that as an extreme statement? Let us think about it for a few moments.

If, at your house, you happen to take a newspaper or a magazine which carries cigaret advertising, and those alluring advertisements tempt you to smoke and try to make you think that it is smart to puff on a cigarette, and if you fall for that temptation, what is the first thing you do?

You brush to one side all the teachings of your parents, your church, and your friends who love you. Instead, you take the advice of a tobacco merchant who has no more interest in you than to get what money he can out of you by making you a slave to his product. And then, you tell yourself, "I think I will buy some cigarets." And so, with a guilty conscience, and feeling as if the eyes of the whole world are upon you, you go and buy your first package of cigarettes. Then you wonder where you are going to smoke them. You do not want to smoke them in front of your parents because you know it is wrong, and you know it would break their hearts. You do not want to smoke in front of your nonsmoking friends because you know what they would tell you. And so, you go some place where neither your friends nor your parents can see you. Then you open the package, and you take out that first cigaret, put it in your mouth, and light it. Then you make a great discovery: You find out that by sucking on one end of that cigaret with the light on the other, you can actually get smoke out of it; and having read what you have in the advertisements, and having puffed away on that cigaret, the whole operation inflates your ego. So you throw back your head, and you blow the smoke in the air, and you say, "Well, I really must be somebody."

You want to smoke some more, inasmuch as you have fallen for that temptation, but you do not want to do it in private all the time, and you do not want to be the only smoker in a nonsmoking crowd, so you seek out other people who smoke, so you can smoke with them. It may be that you already have some smoking friends and that they were the ones who provided those first cigarettes and that you began to smoke with them. In either case, you begin breaking off your connections with your non-smoking friends and start to form your associates among smokers. And in this way, your cigarettes begin to choose your friends for you.

One of the very difficult things about this is that the habits of smokers so often do not stop with smoking, but they include drinking and unwise partying, as well. And when you start going with people who do those things, it will not be very long before you are doing the same things they are, and in that way the cigaret lays the foundation on which you form other evil habits.

If you are going to be a smoker, you realize that you are breaking one of the commandments of God, and you do not feel good about it. You know that over in the ward they speak about the Word of Wisdom every once in a while, and now that you are a smoker you do not like to hear about the Word of Wisdom. You have heard about it all your life, and you do not want your conscience to hurt you any more than it already does, so you tell yourself you had better stay away from your meetings. You begin to realize that for a Latter-day Saint, worship and smoking just do not go together. And so the cigarette persuades you to stay away from church.

When you were small, your parents taught you to pray, and you prayed with more or less regularity all your life. But now that you are a smoker, you feel out of harmony with the Lord and you hesitate to go to him in prayer.

You begin to discover that, for a Latter-day Saint, cigarets undermine faith and interfere with prayer. And as a child who has been hurt avoids the instruments which hurt him, so you with a smarting conscience shy away from your religious duties. You have come to know that spirituality and smoking are incompatible. And so the cigaret persuades you to stop praying.

Your parents also taught you to pay tithing on everything you earned, but now that you do not go to church very often and you are not very proud of your Church connections, you stop paying your tithing. "What is the use?" you ask yourself. You say, "This tithing money itself would buy quite a few cigarets; they cost real money these days." Rather an expensive habit you have picked up! And so the cigaret persuades you to stop paying your tithing.

When you get old enough to get married, you ask yourself, "Whom shall I marry?" If you are a boy you say, "Will it be Helen or Jane or Elizabeth?" And if you are a girl, you ask yourself, "Will it be Tom or Dick or Harry?" And then you tell yourself that you like Tom better than Harry, and Jane better than Elizabeth. And why do you like them better? Because you know them better. And how did you get to know them better?

Because they are in the crowd you go with; you know, the smoking crowd. And they do the things that you do. They are like you. Why, you would not even think of marrying one of your former friends in the non-smoking crowd. How ridiculous! Why, he would not smoke with you—would not even take a cocktail, and he would not neck, and he would not pet, and he would not party around. Why, you would not marry one of them! You are going to marry one of your own crowd. And then, if you want to sit down together and smoke together you can, and there is no embarrassment—so you tell yourself. There is nobody to get after you if you fill the house full of tobacco smoke, and no one to nag at you if your cigaret burns a hole in the overstuffed, or if you drop hot ashes on the new rug. So your cigaret has helped to choose the kind of person you marry.

63

What kind of home will you have? There will not be much faith in it, because the cigarets have already undermined your faith. And you will not say very many prayers because the cigarets have taken care of that too. And there will not be much Church activity in your house, because the cigarets have checked that off also. So you will have a worldly home with precious little of spirituality in it. Is that really the kind of home you want?

Will you have any children in that home? If you are like many of the smoking young people of today, you will not have any children. One of them recently said, "Why a squawking kid would cramp my style! Do you think I am going to stay up and walk the floor in the middle of the night with a squealing baby in my arms? None of that for me." And so the cigaret may help to rob you of one of the greatest blessings that God gives us in this life: The privilege of having little children.

But suppose by some chance you do have children—what will they be like? Why, they will be just like you. They will not believe very much in God, because you will not make religion very important in their lives. They will not say very many prayers because you will not teach them how. And they will not go to church much because you do not. And when they get a little older, they will acquire the other habits that you have, and they will be just about like you. So the cigaret determines in large measure the kind of children you will have.

Do you not see, young people of the Church, how the cigarets can mark out your life for you—point the path for you to follow? Are you, as young Americans, willing to surrender to the tyranny of a cigaret? Are you willing to allow a cigaret to determine in such large measure the kind of life you are going to live? Are you going to allow a cigaret to choose the kind of friends you have, the kind of person you will marry—even the kind of children you may have? Are you, as a young Latter-day Saint, willing to allow a cigarette to determine your attitude toward God?

Let me ask you one other thing: What do you think of religion, anyway? Is it worth while? Is it worth the trouble we go to? Does it do any good in the world? Or would we be better off without it?

I once read an advertisement which asked this question: "How would you like to live in a town in which there were no churches?" And then it listed the crime and the violence and the debauchery and the filth and the heartbreak and the sorrow and the disappointment associated with persons who reject the soul-elevating, character-building influence of true religion. Would you like to live in a town in which there were no churches? Bring it right down to your own case and ask yourself about it. Would you like to live a life in which there was no religion? Do you really want the degrading influence of the irreligious? That influence is just as deadly for an individual as it is for a whole town.

Choose for yourself: Do you want to live a life without God? The cigarette would like you to. But remember, you can never live successfully without the Lord. So many have tried, and all have failed.

And so I come back to the questions with which I began: Have you ever really considered what a cigaret means to a Latter-day Saint? You who smoke now, do not make the mistake of supposing that the Church is against you, because it is not. It only desires your welfare, and it hopes and prays for the day when you will declare your independence from the slavery of nicotine. And you who do not smoke, before you take that first cigaret ask yourself, "Will it help me or hurt me?" Think it over carefully, and may God guide you in your thinking. I earnestly pray for you, in the name of Jesus Christ. Amen. (*Conference Report,* April 1948, pp. 152-56.)

Nicotine: Profile of Peril

By S. S. Field

At a glance, the mother of the two attractive teen-age girls might have been mistaken for either of them. That was yesterday. A glance today reveals a nightmare—a naked body on an autopsy table, its torso bloodsmeared, its face a mask of horror. The scalp has been peeled back like the skin of a grapefruit, and there is only a cavity where a brain once functioned. Death, says the medical report, resulted from a cerebral tumor.

The man was a prominent lawyer in a large southern city. Now he is propped upright in a hospital bed, staring vacantly into space. Into eternity, in fact, for he is dead. "Heart-muscle failure," says the medical certificate.

The wife of the dean of a mid-western community college

comes home from shopping, opens the door to her husband's study—and screams. The dean lies in a muck of blood, his once vital brain making a floral pattern across walls and ceiling. "Self-inflicted gunshot wound," says the coroner's report.

Three deaths, three certifications: cerebral tumor, heart attack, suicide. Yet behind these three seemingly unlike verdicts lies a frightening truth: each of the deaths, in greater or lesser degree, was caused by the same socially acceptable, legally sanctioned drug—a drug that is sold over the counter in 565 *billion* doses a year. The drug is called nicotine, and it comes in the cigarettes that so many of us consume so slavishly. *Had it not been for nicotine, these three deaths might not have occurred.*

In the case of the cerebral tumor, examination of the young mother's brain tissue identified the cancer as a cell type commonly originating in the bronchi of heavy cigarette smokers. From there it spreads easily into the bloodstream, from the lungs through the myriad capillaries of the body, to invade other organs—and the brain is a favorite killing ground. The mother, it should be noted, was a heavy smoker and, as expected, the primary lesion was found in her lung.

In the case of the heart-muscle failure, an autopsy revealed the lawyer's heart to be normal; there was no evidence of thrombosis (clotting). But the man had been ordered not to smoke, because he was under observation for a painful heart condition called angina pectoris. The order was meant to be absolute, for nicotine's "kick" is actually a chemical shock acting on the ganglia of the involuntary nervous system, including the nerves of the heart and arteries. But the lawyer couldn't resist, and had lighted up a forbidden cigarette. Because the man had been heavily addicted to cigarettes, his heart muscle had been sensitized by the nicotine. In this stage of hypersensitivity, an associated spasm of the coronary arteries, caused by nicotine, was sufficient to decrease the blood supply to the sensitized heart muscle and to cause a change from the heart's normal rhythmic beating to a twitching action (ventricular fibrillation). Death followed.

The suicide was an open-and-shut coroner's case. "Death was sudden . . . in ill health for some time," read the tactful obituary. But the dean's family and friends knew that his life had been destroyed by his pathological addiction to nicotine—that his habit had become a form of suicide, and that he had blown off the top of his head when the agony of smoker's emphysema had become too much to bear.

Clearly, nicotine is a dangerous substance. At a seminar on addiction, habituation and the pharmacology of tobacco, held during the 34-nation First World Conference on Smoking and Health in September 1967, there was general concurrence that

65

the presumed action of nicotine "would link smoking dependence with other major forms of dependence, *such as heroin and alcohol.*"

Although most smokers of the 1½ billion cigarettes lighted each day in this country don't realize it, the stimulus they inhale is a volatile, poisonous alkaloid chemically known as $C_{10}H_{14}N_2$ and pharmacologically categorized as an organic nerve drug so powerful that a one-drop injection would cause instant death. In fact, it is believed that *the drug action of nicotine is a primary cause of more deaths each year than are caused by that most frightening of the hard drugs, heroin.*

The possible explanation for nicotine's deadliness is that it may chemically interact in such a way as to open the door to a whole battery of cancer-producing agents, poisons and lung-pollutants in cigarette smoke. On the basis of progressive increases in mortality from cigarette smoking, these substances are now the primary contributory causes of 360,000 *known* deaths a year—an average of 1000 a day.

Among the potentially deadly emissions of cigarette tobacco are at least 7 known and a large number of suspected carcinogenic (cancer-producing) polycyclic hydrocarbons—listed as such by the National Cancer Institute. There are also 15 to 20 volatile substances which are either irritants or poisons, with parts-per-million (ppm) concentrations that are eye-popping. Hydrogen cyanide, for example—one of the deadliest poisons—is present in cigarette smoke in concentrations of 1600 ppm (compared to a "safe" industrial level of 10 ppm). And carbon monoxide has a concentration in cigarette smoke that is at least *1000 times greater* than the allowable environment level.

Today the mortality from cigarette smoking is nearly seven times our annual death toll from highway accidents—a fatality rate that surpasses, in two months, our total loss of American lives during 12 years of the Vietnam war.

So much for the *known* deaths caused by cigarette smoking. What of the *unknown* deaths? Cardiovascular disease, for example, is responsible for more than a million fatalities a year in this country—better than half the total from all causes. According to Dr. Alton Ochsner, head of the famed Ochsner Clinic in New Orleans and one of the world's foremost lung-cancer surgeons, the number of cardiovascular deaths actually caused or provoked by cigarettes—but unrecorded as such—is shockingly high. Dr. Ochsner cites three medical conditions which contribute to this:

Oxygen starvation. The bronchopulmonary diseases—in particular emphysema, which is almost exclusively a smoker's disease—place severe strains on the heart as a result of oxygen deficiency caused by the destruction or congestion of the lung's alveoli, those infinitesimal air sacs in which the carbon-dioxide wastes carried by the blood are replaced with oxygen. At one medical center, pathology reports showed that *30 percent* of the patients diagnosed for congestive heart failure also had emphysema.

Racing heart. Nicotine stimulates an increase in heart rate of as many as 20 beats a minute. This increase may last for as long as 20 minutes after smoking—which for most smokers means as many as *10,000* extra beats a day. That's a punishing amount of extra work for a heart.

Circulatory problems. Nicotine's final blow to the heart is its vasoconstrictive effect. This potent drug causes a convulsive arterial occlusion—actual constriction of the blood vessels—which can produce drops in temperature of fingers and toes of as much as 10° F. with the inhalation of one cigarette.

How serious is the epidemic of death and disablement caused by cigarettes? In 1971, a report from Britain's Royal College of Physicians said: *"Cigarette smoking is now as important a cause of death as were the great epidemic diseases such as typhoid and cholera and tuberculosis that affected previous generations in this country."* Indeed:

All the epidemics of typhoid throughout Western Europe since the beginning of the 16th century have caused fewer estimated deaths than the total known to be caused by cigarettes in one year in the United States alone.

Cigarettes have accounted for more fatalities than were caused by TB epidemics in Europe throughout the 19th century.

The current annual cigarette mortality in this country surpasses the estimated total for all of the known epidemics of yellow fever in history.

What can be done?

First, the time has come to expose a legal absurdity. In 1905, in an alleged political trade involving support of the tobacco-state Congressmen for the Food and Drug Act of 1906, tobacco was removed from the U.S. Pharmacopoeia (listing of drugs), which in effect rendered it immune to control under the Act. Since then, however, several poisonous substances—which *are* controllable—have been found to exist in tobacco smoke in violation of environmental and consumer-protection laws. Clearly, the "immunity" enjoyed by tobaco is illusory.

The facts are, as mentioned earlier, that at least 7 *known* cancer-producing agents and 15 to 20 *known* toxicants are going into the mouths of 56 million people at an average rate of 27 times a day and, 90 percent of the time, directly into their lungs. Tobacco's immunity should be withdrawn.

Second, we need a "completely safe" cigarette law similar to the hazardous-substance laws that ban unsafe ingredients from food, drugs, cosmetics, clothing, children's toys and other household products. In fact, a less hazardous, even perhaps safe cigarette is now entirely feasible. The use of tobacco strains

67

containing little or no nicotine, combined with selective filtration technology, would almost entirely eliminate the dangers of smoking. But it would also eliminate the possible addiction factor which has made cigarette manufacturing so lucrative. The process therefore meets with stiff resistance from the powerful tobacco lobby.

68

The third action is a matter of individual conscience. The Talmud says that "He who saves one life, it is as though he has saved the entire world." Fifty-six million Americans have the opportunity to do just that—by putting out their last cigarette.

(*The Reader's Digest,* September 1973, pp. 77-80. Reprinted with permission. Copyright © 1973 by The Reader's Digest Association, Inc.)

What the Cigarette Commercials Don't Show

(Condensed from Christian Herald)

By Hugh J. Mooney

In cigarette country, television commercials show two or three handsome, rugged cowboys on beautiful horses. Or there are sports cars, planes, or scuba gear. The scene is always one of clean, windswept health. The people have a look of supreme confidence; the lovely girls all smile.

I know another country. It is a land from which few return. In this sad region there are no strong men, no smiling, pretty girls. Executives and store clerks there look very much alike, not only because they wear the same clothes, but because people lying on the raw edge of a thin hope somehow get the same haunted expression on their faces.

I am referring to cancer country. I have been there.

I am 44 years old, and have a wife and two small children. By 1963, I had a comfortable salary with an insurance firm, and the future seemed bright. In May of that year, I developed a slight difficulty in swallowing. Our family physician said that if it persisted for another week, he would arrange an appointment for me with a throat specialist. It did persist. The specialist diagnosed it simply as "a case of nerves"—a diagnosis that he was to reaffirm in October. Finally, in January 1964, convinced that it was more than a case of nerves, I entered a hospital. And there the doctor told me, as gently as he could, that I had cancer of the throat.

The first thing that occurred to me was that I would die and Eileen, my wife, would have to give up the house. What a shame that my children would not be able to grow up in that house! We had bought it only two years before.

The doctor suggested that I enter a well-known Eastern hospital. Two days later, Eileen and I drove there. I was assigned to a four-bed room on the seventh floor of the east wing. This is known as Seven-East.

When I saw the three other patients in my room, I didn't want to believe my eyes. It was suppertime, and the patients were eating. It wasn't much like the television campfire scene. These men stood by their beds and carefully poured a thin pink liquid into small glass tubes. Then they held the tubes high over their heads. The fluid drained down out of the tubes through a thin, clear plastic hose which disappeared into one nostril.

They had to eat this way because throat, mouth, tongue and esophagus had been cut away in surgery. I could actually see the back wall of their gullets—the entire front of the throat was laid open from just below the jaw down almost to the breastbone. Each of them had a large wad of absorbent bandage under his chin to catch the constant flow of saliva pouring out of his throat.

The sight of these "tube feeders" shocked and depressed me more than anything since the day I learned I had cancer. As soon as I had changed into pajamas and robe, I rushed back to the solarium where Eileen was waiting. Shaking, I lit a cigarette and stared about me at all the other patients, some of whom would be dead in a week or so.

The doctor assigned to my case found us there in the solarium. I made it clear to him that I never wanted to become like those other patients. I said that I would rather die than be cut up that way. He told me not to think about it, that perhaps such drastic surgery would not be necessary in my case.

A heavy snow was falling outside. Eileen had to leave to drive the 60 miles home. I walked with her to the elevator, pretending a lot more optimism than I felt. "Drive carefully," I said, and kissed her good-by. The first few hours after the elevator doors closed behind her were probably the worst of my life.

I fled to the solarium, unwilling to face the surgical horrors in my room. Yet everywhere I looked there were patients whose tongues, pharynxes, jaws, throats, chins or noses had been removed. Many of them were waiting for plastic surgery to reconstruct their faces and necks.

For this, it is necessary to grow extra pieces of flesh. Through some sort of surgical miracle these pieces of flesh—called pedicles—can be made to grow anywhere on the patient that the surgeon decides is best. One patient had flesh growing out of the side of his neck in a tubular U, like the handle on a suitcase. Another man had one growing from between his shoulder blades over his right shoulder to a spot in his throat just below the chin. It must have been 18 inches long.

I was torn between horror and pity. What might I look like soon? I reminded myself that surgery might not be necessary, and kept my eyes on the walls, the floor—anywhere but on the other patients.

The television set was on, and the cigarette commercials droned along, extolling the wonderful taste of the product. But these people who had smoked all their lives could no longer taste cigarettes—or anything else. Their food was poured through plastic tubing. There are no tastebuds in plastic tubing.

All the people in the commercials had wonderfully appealing voices, young and vibrant. But the patients around me in the solarium did not have very nice voices. In fact, many had no voice at all; their vocal cords had been cut away.

These voiceless wraiths carried pad and pencil to communicate. Others, whose throat openings had been closed, were able to use an electronic device that looked something like a flashlight. You hold it against your throat, and it picks up vibrations from the section where your vocal cords used to be. It produces a tinny, electronic voice—faint, but understandable.

Next morning, I was taken to the operating room for a bronchoscopic examination. This is very much like swordswallowing. You tilt your head back as far as you can, and doctors slide a metal tube through your mouth and all the way down into your trachea. Your gag reflexes go crazy trying to eject this tube, and you find that it is completely cutting off your supply of air. All this time two or three doctors are taking turns looking down the pipe.

Occasionally they take a sample for a biopsy—lowering something down the tube that snips off a specimen of flesh here and there. I passed out from lack of air during the examination, and came to back on my bed. I was told not to eat or drink anything and to remain in bed for at least two hours.

In an effort to save my voice, so important in insurance work, it was agreed that radiation treatments would be tried. The treatments were not effective, and in August 1964 the doctors told me I would have to undergo surgery.

The night before the operation, knowing that I would never speak again, I tried to tell Eileen how much I loved her and the children. She was very brave. The next morning, on my way to the operating room I remember praying and repeating the name "Jesus" over and over. It seemed somehow right that this should be my last spoken word.

Eleven hours later, I was brought back to my room. Except for an hour in the recovery room, I had spent all that time on the operating table. Next, I learned that the surgeons had removed my larynx, my pharynx, part of my esophagus and a few other random bits and pieces. I was now one of those "surgical freaks" whose appearance had so shocked me some months before. From this time on, I would breathe through a hole at the base of my throat called a stoma.

Knowing how odd my open throat made me appear, I felt completely cut off from humanity—a mere biological specimen. It was a difficult and lonely period of adjustment. Eight subsequent operations were required to reconstruct the front of my neck. Television helped pass the time. All of us there in Seven-East were, I confess, morbidly fascinated by the cigarette commercials. After smoking approximately 19,000 packs of cigarettes, I—we—all—had turned out a bit different from those handsome fellows and beautiful young women.

Young people today are great believers in realism. It might be interesting, therefore, if some advertising agency were to do a cigarette commercial featuring a patient who has lost his throat to cancer caused by smoking. They could choose a man growing one of those flesh pedicles. Or the camera might slowly pan around the room, showing all of us still faithfully smoking brand X or brand Y—those of us who still had a complete mouth to put a cigarette into. They might even show the one total addict I met who smoked by holding his cigarette to the hole that led into his windpipe, through which he breathed air into his lungs.

We don't ride horses or helicopters or sports cars in Seven-East. We ride wheeled tables to the operating room, and if we're lucky we ride them back. Seven-East is only a part of cancer country. They treat lungs on the third floor. I thank God that I have not yet had to visit there. (*Reader's Digest,* January 1968. Used by permission.)

The most damning influence tobacco can have upon a Latter-day Saint is its spiritual consequences. "Wickedness never was happiness," said a Nephite prophet. (Alma 46:10.) If one does not believe it is wicked or sinful to smoke, he should ask himself. "Does the use of tobacco injure, hurt, cause illness, or even death?" Man has learned from scientific studies and experimental research that many illnesses, ofttimes excruciating pain, and death can result from the use of tobacco. The Lord has given the Word of Wisdom to warn man against injury to his body, and so that man might maintain spiritual communion with his Heavenly Father.

The deleterious results from breaking this commandment was expressed by President George Albert Smith while he was serving as a member of the Council of the Twelve:

I want to say to you, in my judgment, that the use of tobacco, a little thing as it seems to some men, has been the means of destroying their spiritual life, has been the means of driving from them the companionship of the Spirit of our Father, has alienated them from the society of good men and women, and has brought upon them the disregard and reproach of the children that have been born to them, and yet the devil will say to a man, Oh, it's only a little thing! (*Conference Report,* April 1918, p. 40.)

72

8

Hot Drinks
Are Not for the Body or Belly

I said to the Saints at our last annual Conference, the Spirit whispers to me to call upon the Latter-day Saints to observe the Word of Wisdom, to let tea, coffee, and tobacco alone, and to abstain from drinking spirituous drinks. This is what the Spirit signifies through me. If the Spirit of God whispers this to His people through their leader, and they will not listen nor obey, what will be the consequence to their disobedience? Darkness and blindness of mind with regard to the things of God will be their lot; they will cease to have the spirit of prayer, and the spirit of the world will increase in them in proportion to their disobedience until they apostatize entirely from God and His ways. (Brigham Young, *Journal of Discourses*, 12:117, August 17, 1867.)

This statement from the second president of The Church of Jesus Christ of Latter-day Saints establishes a fundamental principle of the gospel known to all knowledgeable Latter-day Saints. Obedience to the counsel of the Lord's prophets is the way to enjoy the Spirit of the Lord. In the above instruction one should notice that tea and coffee are listed as a part of the Word of Wisdom to be obeyed if one expects to receive the blessings of the gospel. In the early days of this dispensation, some members of the Church did not feel that the Lord prohibited the use of tea and coffee as a part of his plan for the welfare of his people.

Among Latter-day Saints today, however, there is no question as to the meaning of hot drinks (D&C 89:9), although tea and coffee are not mentioned specifically in the revelation. Without a specific definition of the term "hot drinks," early members of the Church might have concluded, as we might today, that it referred to drinks served at high temperatures.

On a Sabbath day in July of 1833, five months after the revelation was received, Joel H. Johnson was present when he heard the Prophet Joseph Smith ask the congregation, "Now, what do we drink when we take our meals?

"Tea and coffee. Is it not?" "Then they are what the Lord meant when He said 'hot drinks.' " (Joel H. Johnson, *Voice from the Mountains*, p. 12.)

The following definition from Hyrum Smith, the Prophet's brother and Patriarch to the Church, provides the answer: "And again, 'hot drinks are not for the body, or belly;' there are many who wonder what this can mean; whether it refers to tea or coffee, or not. I say it does refer to tea, and coffee." (*Times and Seasons*, 3:800.)

On October 30, 1870, President Brigham Young said: "I have heard it argued that tea and coffee are not mentioned therein; that is very true; but what were the people in the habit of taking as hot drinks when that revelation was given? Tea and coffee. We were not in the habit of drinking water very hot, but tea and coffee—the beverages in common use." (*Journal of Discourses*, 13:277.)

Medical men expressed varying opinions throughout the nineteenth century regarding the effects of tea and coffee, some believing they were beneficial while others thought they were injurious. The writer of a textbook on health and the human body in 1866 extolled the virtues of tea and coffee in daily diet:

> Tea and coffee form prominent constituents in the daily diet of the majority of the inhabitants of the globe. They are possessed of considerable power as nervous stimulants, and are pleasant beverages. It has been satisfactorily demonstrated that they not only act as direct stimulants when taken after the performance of fatiguing works, but also prevent the waste of tissues during labor, and are therefore of value from an economic point of view.
> . . .
> Coffee is both tonic and exhilarant, and is held in high esteem by the student; it is regarded as an intellectual stimulant, and has been the brain food of many distinguished authors and literateurs. When freshly made, and taken in small quantity after a meal it assists digestion; but it should not be used in excess, or mingled with sugar or milk, as it is then apt to produce indigestion. (John C. Draper, *A Textbook on Anatomy, Physiology and Hygiene*, New York: Harper and Brothers, 1866, pp. 250-51.)

A wise and instructive understanding concerning the expression "hot drinks" was made by the authors of a well-known book on the Word of Wisdom:

That the expression "hot drinks" was used in the Word of
Wisdom rather than "coffee and tea," is notable; for by so doing
a host of other injurious habit-forming beverages now used (or
that may be used) become subject to the Word of Wisdom.
Indeed, the use of the words "hot drinks" implies a knowledge
beyond that possessed by man when the Word of Wisdom was
received. It is remarkable indeed that Joseph Smith could so
boldly declare himself against coffee and tea, as against all
similar hurtful beverages, at a time when the world's learning
could not safely make the statement.

75

Human experience, since that day, is all against the use of
coffee and tea, and similar beverages. They gradually influence
harmfully the mind and the body of the user, especially if excesses
are indulged in, and the tendency of the habit is to demand more
and more. (Widtsoe, *The Word of Wisdom, A Modern Interpretation*,
rev. ed., 1950, pp. 89-90.)

Caffeine, the principal ingredient of coffee and tea, is a
poison similar to strychnine. In an article in *Science Digest*,
Dr. Irwin Ross wrote: "An infinitesimal amount applied
directly to your brain would send your body into uncon-
trollable convulsions. Injected into your muscles, it would
paralyze them." ("What Coffee Really Does to You,"
Science Digest, July 1966.) Dr. Ross indicated that these violent things do not happen to the coffee drinker, because
most of the caffeine goes straight to the kidneys and is
promptly excreted. However, things do happen to the body
when one drinks one or two cups of coffee, such as:

Within a few minutes . . . there's an increase of up to 400
percent in the stomach's secretion of hydrochloric acid. Your
salivary glands double their output; your heart beats 15 percent
faster; your lungs work 13 percent harder. Blood vessels get
narrower in your brain, wider in and around your heart. Your
metabolism rate goes up to 25 percent; your kidneys manufacture
and excrete up to 100 percent more urine. (Ibid.)

A nationwide survey conducted a few years ago by the
Pan American Coffee Bureau revealed that 96 percent of
the families in the United States drink coffee every day.
Eight out of ten adults drink it daily, as do one in four
children. Consumption of coffee increased about 50

percent more in 1966 than in the ten years before. It is estimated that Americans drink annually a billion more gallons of coffee than milk. (Ibid.)

Despite the fact that coffee is the number one drink in the United States (tea is consumed much less), not a great deal of research on its effects has been done. One of the difficulties in this research is in distinguishing between the effects of tobacco use and coffee and tea consumption, since practically every tobacco user also drinks coffee, and most coffee drinkers also use tobacco.

About fifty years ago the first comprehensive research on the long-range effects of coffee drinking was conducted by the Massachusetts Institute of Technology at the request of the coffee industry. The final report maintained that there was no convincing evidence that "coffee is prejudicial to the health of the general public," but a small percentage of the public "responds unfavorably to caffeine stimulants." (Amy Selwyn, "Coffee: Pickup or Poison?" *Pageant Magazine*, December 1950.)

The Lord declared over 100 years ago that "hot drinks" are not good. In addition to the immediate effects of caffeine drinks already noted, what are the injurious effects of consuming these drinks? Research on the effects of caffeine in beverages is still in its infancy and, as Latter-day Saints have learned, the Lord's word is vindicated by the passage of time. But what is the situation today?

Some fifty years ago it was believed that coffee aided in the digestive process. This is not true today. (Dr. Irwin Ross, *op. cit.*) Regular use of coffee often causes stomach discomfort. In one study several hundred non-coffee drinkers drank two to six cups of coffee daily for several months, and 50 percent complained of painful burning sensations in their stomachs, nausea, and excessive gas. When they stopped drinking coffee, their stomach problems disappeared. (Ibid.)

Stomach ulcer patients are generally advised to stop using all beverages containing caffeine, including coffee, tea, and cola. These beverages cause the stomach to release hydrochloric acid, and excess acid causes ulcers; however, the addition of cream to coffee does reduce the secretion of the acid flow. ("How Coffee Affects Your Health," *Today's Health*, April 1967.)

A study of stomach and esophagus cancer patients in a New York hospital revealed that one in four of the patients had been in the habit of drinking very hot beverages. There was no conclusive evidence that hot coffee does cause cancer; however, studies have shown that there is much more gastric cancer in the United States than in England, where most beverages are drunk lukewarm. (Dr. Irwin Ross, *op. cit.*)

Studies on caffeine in beverages indicates that for some people serious harm may not result from such drinks, but for those with certain diseases, such beverages are definitely injurious. For example, excessive use can cause overstimulation of the nervous system, resulting in overexcitability, insomnia, or tremors. ("Caffeine: Grounds for Concern?" *Consumer Reports*, January 1971.)

Is coffee a stimulant? A common practice in business is to allow employees to have a coffee break during the morning and afternoon, usually to pep them up and increase their skills. While some mental stimulation may result from the use of caffeine beverages, many authorities believe that drinking more than two cups of coffee results in lessened mental acuity. Excessive coffee drinking is often found among persons in certain occupations where the taking of a stimulant is believed essential, such as truck drivers, actors, and people who work at night. One researcher determined that the best advice for such people is a walk break rather than a coffee break. ("Coffee and Your Health," *Consumer Bulletin*, April 1971.)

Do caffeine beverages disturb one's sleep? This depends upon the amount consumed. An authority on sleep has stated that it takes at least two cups of coffee to spoil one's sleep, and the idea that it is a matter of the mind does not agree with his research. (Dr. Irwin Ross, *op. cit.*)

What about persons with diabetes? It is believed that in some diabetics, the amount of blood sugar can be increased by the caffeine in two cups of black coffee. Even latent diabetics are warned that caffeine drinks are not good. ("Caffeine: Grounds for Concern?" *Consumer Reports*, January 1971.)

Does coffee contribute to heart disease? The answer to this question is not yet clear, for there has been some conflicting information over the years. A study at a Western Electric Company plant compared persons who had coronary heart disease with a non-coronary group. To a significant degree those in the coronary group were coffee drinkers, though this fact cannot necessarily be construed to mean that coffee drinking causes or contributes to heart disease. ("Coffee and Your Heart," *Science Digest*, October 1963.)

A more recent study concluded that "coffee drinking, as engaged in by the general population, is not a factor in the development of atherosclerotic cardiovascular disease [heart disease resulting from hardening of the coronary arteries]." ("Coffee and Cardiovascular Disease, Observations from the Framington Study," *New England Journal of Medicine*, October 24, 1974.) The authors indicated that their study did not consider the possible effect of coffee intake on existing cardiovascular disease. (Ibid.) Their report, however, provides the reader with some important possible effects of coffee drinking:

> It is not illogical to consider the effect of coffee ingestion a possible agent in the development of atherosclerosis [hardening of the coronary arteries] and to examine its relation to risk factors such as hypertension [high blood pressure], glucose intolerance [sugar intolerance], hyperlipidemia [high blood fat levels], cardiac-muscle metabolism [heart muscle], and myocardial irritability [heart muscle irritability]. Coffee has been labeled a proarrhythmic [irregularity in the rhythm of the heart's beating] and by implication a possible factor in sudden death due to fatal arrhythmia. Coffee can produce a slight rise in blood pressure and pulse rate, may interfere with adequate sleep in some people, and is a mild cerebral stimulant. Repeated stimulation by coffee could conceivably have an adverse effect on the cardiovascular system. Removal of the caffeine eliminates all the effects noted above. (Ibid.)

With one in four children using coffee and the coffee

78

industry working to increase coffee consumption, it is important to know what doctors say about its use by children. The chief argument of the industry is that since most children drink other beverages containing caffeine, why shouldn't they drink coffee? Two hundred pediatricians were polled as to their feelings on giving coffee to children. Only one of them said there was no reason why not. (Dr. Irwin Ross, *op. cit.*)

79

Common drinks and foods that contain caffeine, in addition to coffee and tea, include cola drinks, cocoa, and any food containing chocolate. Analyses of these drinks and foods have shown that coffee contains the greatest concentration of caffeine. In the order of their caffeine content the ranking would be: coffee and tea (about the same), cola drinks ("the Food and Drug Administration requires that if a drink is labeled 'cola,' it must contain some caffeine, but not more than about 50 milligrams per 10-ounce bottle," and solid chocolate bars. ("Caffeine: Grounds for Concern?" *Consumer Reports*, January 1971; "Coffee and Your Health," *Consumer Bulletin*, April 1971.)

The prophets of the Church have never included the other caffeine drinks and foods as a requirement for obeying the Word of Wisdom for certain purposes. A *Church News* editorial declared:

> When interviewing for temple recommends, for instance, or for advancement in the priesthood, or for baptism, or for any other purpose, bishops never inquire as to whether a person drinks cocoa or eats chocolate candy. If the use of cocoa and chocolate were against the doctrine of the Church such inquiry would be made, but it is not. (*Church News*, May 5, 1962, p. 16.)

The same information given also includes cola drinks.

Americans are more and more turning to drugs, many of which are harmful when misused, used to excess, or without following a physician's advice. (For valuable advice on this subject, see Ewart A. Swinyard, "Wisdom in All Things," *New Era*, September 1974.) In recent years the use and effects of mind-destroying and health-debilitating drugs, such as marijuana, heroin, and LSD, have received considerable publicity. Testimonies of drug addicts and users are filled with sorrow and regret. Crimes of every description have been committed in order to satisfy the addict's craving for drugs. Loss of mental and physical powers and even death have resulted from tampering with drugs.

80

Even drugs that seem harmless are being used to excess. President Spencer W. Kimball declared at the October 1974 general conference:

> We hope our people will eliminate from their lives all kinds of drugs so far as possible. Too many depend upon drugs as tranquilizers and sleep helps, which is not always necessary.
> Certainly numerous young people have been damaged or destroyed by the use of marijuana and other deadly drugs. We deplore such. (*Conference Report*, October 1974, p. 6.)

The use of any drug that is habit-forming is contrary to the Word of Wisdom. The drug user loses self-respect and thus lowers himself in the eyes of God and man. Could this possibly be construed as wisdom? Not when one knows the high status of his spirit birth as a child of God.

President Joseph Fielding Smith gave the following counsel as a safe guide to follow:

> If in doubt as to any food or drink, whether it is good or harmful, let it alone until you have learned the truth in regard to it. If anything offered is habit-forming, we will be safe in concluding that it contains some ingredients that are harmful to the body and should be avoided. (*Improvement Era*, February 1956, p. 79.)

This counsel was given in answer to the question, "Why does not the Lord give us further revelation to cover the many other stimulants and drinks and the proper foods for the body?" President Smith wrote:

> The answer is because such revelation is unnecessary. The Word of Wisdom is a basic law. It points the way and gives us ample instruction in regard to both food and drink, good for the body and also detrimental. If we sincerely follow what is written with the aid of the Spirit of the Lord, we need no further counsel. (Ibid., p. 78.)

In a world of stress when every advantage—mental, emotional, and physical—is needed to cope with life's problems, Latter-day Saints are blessed richly with revealed knowledge on how to have health commensurate with the needs of the day. They know that the Lord is ever mindful of the well-being of his children who are obedient to his commandments.

9

Positive Aspects
of the Word of Wisdom

Prepare to die, is not the exhortation in this church and kingdom; but prepare to live is the word with us, and improve all we can in this life that we may be the better prepared to enjoy a better life hereafter, wherein we may enjoy a more exalted condition of intelligence, wisdom, light, knowledge, power, and glory, and exaltation. Then let us seek to extend the present life to the uttermost, by observing every law of health. . . . (Brigham Young, *Journal of Discourses*, 11:32, August 1-10, 1865.)

The word of the Lord to this generation is clear as to the foods that will sustain life and give health. In the Word of Wisdom we read:

And again, verily I say unto you, all wholesome herbs God hath ordained for the constitution, nature, and use of man—
Every herb in the season thereof, and every fruit in the season thereof; all these to be used with prudence and thanksgiving.
Yea, flesh also of beasts and of the fowls of the air, I, the Lord, have ordained for the use of man with thanksgiving; nevertheless they are to be used sparingly;
And it is pleasing unto me that they should not be used, only in times of winter, or of cold, or famine.
All grain is ordained for the use of man and of beasts, to be the staff of life, not only for man but for the beasts of the field, and the fowls of heaven, and all wild animals that run or creep on the earth;
And these hath God made for the use of man only in times of famine and excess of hunger.
All grain is good for the food of man; as also the fruit of the vine; that which yieldeth fruit, whether in the ground or above the ground—
Nevertheless, wheat for man. . . . (D&C 89:10-17.)

A summary of these verses provides us with the following: herbs (vegetables), fruits, meat, and all grains, especially wheat. Although these foods are basic in the diet of man, depending upon where he lives, the *emphasis* as well as the *limitations* for their use gives us one of the major contributions of the revelation.

In the days of King Nebuchadnezzar of Babylon, the people of the kingdom of Judah were taken captive. Among them was Daniel, a prince, who, with other young men of skill, was brought to the palace to be taught the learning and language of the Chaldeans. When he was offered food that the Lord had commanded the Jews not to eat, he asked the chief officer of the palace to give him and his companions food that they had been commanded to eat. The chief officer felt that if he permitted their request, it might appear to the king that they were not being cared for properly, and he might be punished. However, Daniel persuaded him to allow them to eat their own food for ten days, and at the conclusion of that period, they looked healthier than those who ate the food of the Chaldeans. Daniel and his companions fared well on the food the Lord had commanded them to eat, and they grew in wisdom and understanding, even ten times better than the king's wise men. (See Daniel 1.)

In giving them laws for their welfare, the Lord has been mindful of his people in all ages, taking into consideration the conditions under which they have lived and their places of residence. We live under law, and if we violate certain laws, we must pay the penalty. (See D&C 88:36-39.) Disobedience to the laws of health brings ill health. The Lord expects that Latter-day Saints will keep themselves in good health so they may find greater happiness and more opportunities to assist in the building up of the kingdom of God.

Considerable emphasis has been placed upon the don'ts of the Word of Wisdom, and those who hear only what may be termed the negative aspects of this law, such as non-use of tea, coffee, tobacco, alcohol, and other harmful habit-forming drugs may think that the Word of Wisdom consists only of those prohibitions. However, there are many positive aspects in the Word of Wisdom.

When the Lord commanded man to keep the Sabbath day holy, he promised many blessings to those who keep his commandments. He said:

Verily I say, that inasmuch as ye do this, the fulness of the

83

earth is yours, the beasts of the field and the fowls of the air, and that which climbeth upon the trees and walketh upon the earth;

Yea, and the good things which come of the earth, whether for food or for raiment, or for houses, or for barns, or for orchards, or for gardens, or for vineyards;

Yea, all things which come of the earth, in the season thereof, are made for the benefit and the use of man, both to please the eye and to gladden the heart;

Yea, for food and for raiment, for taste and for smell, to strengthen the body and to enliven the soul.

And it pleaseth God that he hath given all these things unto man; for unto this end were they made to be used, with judgment, not to excess, neither by extortion. (D&C 59:16-20.)

Food is to be used with "judgment, not to excess." The American people have often been accused of eating too much. The need for calories decreases as one grows older, because the basal metabolism requirement is lower and total activity is decreased. If the same diet is continued as was used in earlier life, the extra calories ingested produce body fat, resulting in weight increase. (*Food,* The Yearbook of Agriculture, United States Department of Agriculture, 1959, p. 315.)

Reason would suggest that the word *herbs* in the Word of Wisdom refers to plants and vegetables, which are not mentioned by name. In fact, a century ago the word *herbs* included plants and vegetables. Addition of the modifying words "all wholesome" indicates that all edible vegetables and fruits of earth are included in the revelation; it also indicates that some are not to be used as food. (Widtsoe, *The Word of Wisdom, A Modern Interpretation,* p. 120.)

The revelation says that herbs and fruits are to be used "in the season thereof." Several meanings have been ascribed to this expression, all of which seem to pertain to good health rules. John A. and Leah D. Widtsoe gave us a definition that confirms the Word of Wisdom, because the function of vitamins in the human body was unknown when the revelation was received; the science of modern nutrition, which provides us with information about what we should eat to maintain good health, was developed after the Prophet Joseph Smith lived. They write:

84

... it is now known that there are substances in all *fresh* foods which if present, bring health and, if absent, cause disease and ultimate death. These vital substances have been named vitamins. ... This is a mjaor discovery of modern nutritional science. ... (Ibid., pp. 139-40.)

Vitamins are essential in certain amounts for the following purposes: growth and reproduction, formation of antibodies, coagulation of the blood, resistance to infection, and soundness of bones, teeth, skin, blood, and nervous tissue. With enzymes they function in innumerable chemical reactions concerned with the metabolism of food.

Some persons have assumed that the expression "in the season thereof" means that fruits and vegetables are to be used only in the season of their growth. President Joseph Fielding Smith wrote: "This is not the intent, but any grain or fruit is out of season no matter what part of the year it may be, if it is unfit for use." (*Church History and Modern Revelation,* 1953, 1:385.)

Church authorities have never interpreted "in the season thereof" to exclude canned foods, recognizing that this process is necessary to preserve food for future use, but fresh fruits and vegetables should be used when available. (Widtsoe, *The Word of Wisdom, A Modern Interpretation,* p. 144.)

Several questions regarding canned foods have been answered by the U.S. Department of Agriculture:

Does canning destroy the nutritive value of fruit and vegetables? Good commercial canning methods cause relatively little loss.

Are home-canned foods as nutritious as commercially canned foods? It depends. Foods of high quality canned at home under favorable conditions retain their nutrients well, but home operators and methods vary so much that it is not possible to make definite comparisons. See Home and Garden Bulletin No. 8, "Home Canning of Fruits and Vegetables."

In canned vegetables and fruit, are the nutrients in the food or in the liquid? Soluble nutrients are about evenly distributed throughout the contents of the can. Drained solids make up about two-thirds of the contents; therefore, about two-thirds of the soluble nutrients would be in the food and one-third in the liquid.

Is it safe to leave canned foods in the can? Yes. The can is an excellent container, but food in [opened] cans should have the same care as fresh-cooked foods and be kept in a refrigerator.

Do canned fruits and vegetables lose food value on the pantry shelf? Very little, if the storage place is cool. In a year, foods stored at a temperature under 65° F. show a small loss of ascorbic acid and thiamine, ranging from 10 to 15 percent. However, when stored at temperatures up to 80° F. the loss doubles, increasing to 25 percent. The loss continues as the storage period lengthens.

Does freezing affect the nutritive values of fruit and vegetables? Foods of high quality, frozen by good methods, retain their nutrients well. Blanching before freezing causes some loss of vitamins and minerals. (*Consumers All*, The Yearbook of Agriculture, 1965, p. 411.)

There is no answer to the question, What specific characteristics make a fruit or a vegetable most desirable? However, the U.S. Department of Agriculture indicates that high-quality fruit and vegetables must be unspoiled by diseases, insects, mechanical injury, or contamination from foreign matter. Also, most fruits must be ripe, and products must be "fresh or properly stored or preserved if they are to possess their respective desirable properties." In general a person develops preferences for that to which he becomes accustomed. The factors that influence one's judgment of excellence include color, texture, consistency, flavor, and aroma. One's prejudices regarding these attributes determine how good the fruit or vegetable is, though they do not have any relationship to nutritive value, and it has been felt that few consumers pay much attention to the nutritive value of the fruits and vegetables they choose.

Therefore, if we are to be concerned about "what is good for us"—as well as with what is merely "good"—we need to give attention to the properties in these foods that are associated with high vitamin content—the degree of yellow or orange and green color and their freshness or state of preservation. (*Food*, The Yearbook of Agriculture, 1959, p. 374.)

Fruits and vegetables are a major source of vitamins and minerals. Citrus fruits, strawberries, cantaloupes, vegetables of the cabbage family, and numerous other fruits and vegetables contain an abundance of ascorbic

86

acid (vitamin C). Succulent (juicy) vegetables and most fruits have a high water content and only small amounts of energy-yielding nutrients. A head of lettuce may be 95 percent water and have some minerals and vitamins, with more in the darker green leaves than in the bleached inner parts. On the other hand, potatoes, sweet potatoes, and bananas have less water but more carbohydrates than do lettuce and other leafy or tender vegetables. Except for avocados, fruits and vegetables have generally very small amounts of fat. "The orange-colored and dark green products, like carrots, broccoli, spinach, turnip greens, and some varieties of sweet potatoes, have particularly high vitamin A values." (*Food for Us All,* The Yearbook of Agriculture, 1969, p. 316.) Four or more servings daily of fruits and vegetables are recommended.

Today, over 140 years after the Word of Wisdom was received, we understand better than did our forebears what the Lord meant by the phrase "in the season thereof" as it concerns the eating of fruits and vegetables. They are essential in maintaining health. But though the science of nutrition has given us guidance on what is best consumed for good health, this does not mean that a perfectly balanced menu is universally available and that all would use it.

If some superdietitian could hand everyone a simple, perfectly balanced menu and get them to use it, much as a farmer feeds his cows, it would be a comparatively simple matter to have everyone well nourished. But it would be an unfortunate state of affairs, because we would then be cows or robots instead of human beings. As human beings, we expect to get emotional satisfactions from food as well as to meet our physical needs. These emotional satisfactions are often tied up with our habits, and we resist changes that we think might interfere with them. This is one reason why the problem of nutrition is complicated, as every mother knows if she has tried to teach a child to eat properly. (*Food,* The Yearbook of Agriculture, 1959, p. 329.)

The Word of Wisdom states that "all grain is good for the food of man." Cereals, which are major foods throughout most of the world, are relatively high in protein. All foodstuffs contain carbon, hydrogen, and oxygen in varying proportions; because proteins also contain nitrogen, they have special importance and power. Without proteins, life would not be possible. (Ibid., p. 57.) When one has too little protein, the fluid balance of the body is upset so that the tissues hold abnormal amounts of liquid and become swollen.

88

The proteins in the body tissues are not there as fixed, unchanging substances deposited for a lifetime of use. They are in a constant state of exchange. Some molecules or parts of molecules always are breaking down and others are being built as replacements. This exchange is a basic characteristic of living things; in the body it is referred to as the dynamic state of body constituents—the opposite of a static or fixed state. This constant turnover explains why our diet must supply adequate protein daily even when we no longer need it for growth. The turnover of protein is faster within the cells of a tissue (intracellular) than in the substance between the cells (intercellular).

Proteins, like starches, sugars, and fats, can supply energy. (*Food,* The Yearbook of Agriculture, 1959, p. 58.)

Cereal grains, especially wheat, are also an important source of carbohydrates, which give us energy; and they help the body use fat more efficiently. (Ibid, p. 88.) Wheat is a staple food in the United States and in the temperate zone, while rice and other cereal grains are more commonly used in other climates.

Some persons have suggested that if one lives the Word of Wisdom, he will not eat white bread and some other products that are commercially processed. However, the revelation does not specifically prohibit the use of such products as white flour, cocoa, chocolate, and white sugar, while it does prohibit or has been interpreted by the prophets to prohibit the use of tea, coffee, tobacco, and alcoholic beverages. President David O. McKay advised the Saints to take the Word of Wisdom as the Lord gave it, indicating that one is not violating the Word of Wisdom by eating white bread. (*Pathways to Happiness,* p. 110.)

An editorial in the *Church News* declared:

Persons who say that it is against the Word of Wisdom to eat white flour simply do not know what they are talking about. The same thing is true with respect to white sugar. The Church has never banned or even raised a question about either one. Only unauthorized persons who speak on their own responsibility try to make Church doctrine out of their private personal views. (May 5, 1962.)

The following information debunks belief that nutri-   89
tive value is destroyed by commercial food processing and cooking:

Foods such as white flour, refined cereal, canned food, and even pasteurized milk are condemned by the food faddist. He bemoans the supposed extensive loss in vitamins because of warehousing, storage, and exposure to daylight and insists that there is nothing left of any nutritional value after the food has been cooked. . . .
He does not tell you that modern food processing methods have been designed to produce foods of high nutritional value. Fruit and vegetables are canned or frozen at the peak of their nutritional value, and flour, bread, milk, and margarine are all nutritionally improved in accord with recommendations of authorities on nutrition.
A certain percentage of raw fruit and vegetables is desirable in the diet, but most of our common foods usually are served cooked because they are more palatable and because they are more easily digested. (*Consumers All,* The Yearbook of Agriculture, 1965, p. 404.)

What about nutrients added to food? The following answers to questions of consumers are revealing:

Is whole-wheat flour more nutritious than plain white flour? Yes. Whole-wheat flour is milled to include all parts of the wheat kernel, including the germ and outer layers, in which some nutrients are highly concentrated. White flour is milled from the endosperm, which is mainly starch. Enrichment of white flour is common now.
What is enriched flour? Enriched flour is refined flour to which certain vitamins and minerals are added within limits stipulated by law. Enrichment has led to great improvement in the American diet.
Are there other foods with added nutrients? Yes, many. The first important addition of an essential nutrient to a staple article of food was addition of iodine to table salt in 1924. Vitamin A may be added to margarine in amounts set by Federal law and vitamin D to milk according to Federal and State laws. Many

other foods have nutrients added in amounts that are not
regulated by law. Many breakfast cereals, particularly those in
ready-to-serve form, have added nutrients. Ingredients added to
foods for which there are no regulations as to amounts must be
named on the label.

Are commercial breads as nutritious as the old-fashioned loaf? Yes. In
fact, today's commercial recipes have improved the nutritive
value of white bread over that of the twenties. (Ibid., p. 412.)

Meat is good for man, said the Lord in an earlier
revelation, and "whoso forbiddeth to abstain from meats,
that man should not eat the same, is not ordained of God.
For, behold, the beasts of the field and fowls of the air, . . .
are ordained for the use of man. . . ." (D&C 49:18-19.)

Elder and Sister Widtsoe advised the following: "The
Word of Wisdom does not contain a prohibition against
meat eating, but urges its sparing use. Unfortunately, this
advice is not generally observed, and man's health suffers
in consequence. Many people eat too much meat; a few do
not eat enough." (*The Word of Wisdom*, p. 260.)

An informative answer to the question "Can vegetable
protein be substituted for animal protein?" indicates that a
small amount of animal protein is necessary to supplement
vegetable protein and amino acids essential for tissue
building:

Vegetable proteins generally are of lower quality than
animal proteins because they fail to provide the complete
assortment of amino acids in the amounts the body needs for
tissue building. Certain foods of plant origin—soybeans, nuts, dry
beans, and peas—are better than others from plants. It takes only
a small amount of protein from animal sources, however, to
supplement the protein in vegetable foods. Combinations like
cereal and milk, macaroni and cheese, egg and bread, and beans
and frankfurters provide better protein than foods of plant origin
used alone. (*Food,* The Yearbook of Agriculture, 1959, p. 24.)

Other answers to questions bearing on this general subject are informative:

*Is bread that is advertised as high-protein bread a good substitute for
meat?* No. Many of the breads advertised as "high-protein" bread
contain very little more protein than ordinary bread. Four slices
of the ordinary white bread contain less than half as much

protein as in an average serving of lean meat (2 to 3 ounces cooked). The protein in bread must be combined with some protein from foods of animal origin in order to provide all of the amino acids needed by the body.

What can we eat to give us protein and few calories? Good sources of protein that are relatively low in fat and thus in calories are skim milk, cottage cheese, eggs, lean meat and fish, chicken, and turkey.

91

How does the protein content of peanut butter compare with that of meat? Four tablespoons of peanut butter supply about the same amount of protein as 2 ounces of lean cooked meat (without bone).

What are some cheap meat substitutes? Common meat alternates include poultry, fish, eggs, dry beans and peas, and cheese. Dry beans and peas are likely to be the cheapest of these foods on the basis of cost per serving. Cheese like the cottage, Swiss, and Cheddar-type may be more economical to buy than many cuts of meat—also poultry and eggs, especially when they are in plentiful supply. Certain fish, depending on the locality and supply, are inexpensive.

The cost of meat varies with the cut, quality, and kind of meat. You may find that some meats are as inexpensive as certain alternates. (Ibid., pp. 25-27.)

Nutritionists agree that one's daily menu should include a variety of foods to maintain good health. It is sometimes assumed, because of great emphasis upon vitamin and mineral capsules sold over the counter, these may be sufficient.

Why can't I eat and drink whatever I please and take vitamin and mineral capsules to make sure I get essential nutrients? A diet chosen by chance is not safe. It may lack protein and energy and other essential nutrients. It may supply too much carbohydrates and not enough of the other essentials. Vitamin and mineral preparations cannot take the place of the food sources of nutrients. (*Food,* The Yearbook of Agriculture, 1959, p. 26.)

For the purpose of making available information on daily food suggestions from the Department of Agriculture, chapter 10 includes their recommendations as well as answers to many questions regarding nutrition.

In the revelation on the Word of Wisdom we read: "Nevertheless, wheat for man, and corn for the ox, and oats for the horse, and rye for the fowls and for swine, and for all beasts of the field, and barley for all useful animals, and for mild drinks, as also other grain." (D&C 89:17.)

Recent information indicates that the cattle ("ox") industry uses corn as the primary grain for feeding cattle of all types. In fact, in 1968, 97 million tons of corn were used for feeding livestock in the United States, whereas, four million tons of wheat were used. (*Feed Situation*, U.S. Department of Agriculture, November 1968, p. 17.)

Oats are considered to be an excellent feed for horses, and dehulled oats (with the fibrous outer coat removed) are high in protein.

Barley is also used for all types of livestock and is particularly valuable in feeding beef and dairy cattle, while rye is used as feed for swine and poultry.

Thus we see that modern nutritional findings and practices substantiate what has been known to Latter-day Saints for nearly a century and a half through revelation.

President Joseph Fielding Smith wrote the following regarding the positive aspects of the Word of Wisdom:

We seldom hear of the things mentioned which are "ordained for the constitution, nature, and use of man." The Lord has given us all good herbs, fruits, and grains. These are to be the main foods of men, beast, and fowls. But we should not overlook the fact that they are to be used with "prudence and thanksgiving." In another revelation (Sec. 59) we are told they are not to be used "to excess, neither by extortion." The difficulty with most of the human family, is eating too much, and failing to heed this counsel. There would be less disease and mankind would live longer if all would also heed the counsel of the Lord concerning the use of wholesome foods. Many a man thinks he keeps the Word of Wisdom, who knows only the "don'ts," which are but a part of its great meaning. (*Church History and Modern Revelation*, 1:385.)

We have talked about some of the "do's" of the Word of Wisdom. This chapter continues this important aspect of the Word of Wisdom with information from an authoritative source, the United States Department of Agriculture. Some selected questions and answers from the USDA regarding foods and nutrients and food quackery are also included.

The Foods You Eat

By Ruth M. Leverton

The foods you eat are more important to your health than the facts you know about nutrition. What you know may or may not influence what you eat, but what you eat does influence what you can do and how you feel.

93

It is easy to know more about nutrition than you may care to know, and it is easy to know more about it than you understand. Just as you can travel by air without being trained in aeronautics, you can be well nourished without being a specialist in nutrition science.

Nutrition does not mean eating food you do not like because it is good for you. Nutrition means how your body uses the food you eat for your well-being, health, vigor. Nutrition does not mean that eating should be a chore, a routine, a matter of bookkeeping and counting.

People may differ in how much they want to know about nutrition, but everyone needs to know a few facts about food and health as a basis for his decisions about the food he eats and thus the level of nutritional well-being he will have.

We need food to give us energy to move, breathe, keep the heart beating, keep warm, and help in growth and upkeep.

Energy is a necessity, but we need food for other reasons, too. Food supplies a complete variety of substances—nutrients—that are essential for building, upkeep, and repair and for keeping the body running in an efficient, orderly way.

Science knows at least 50 nutrients, each of which has special jobs to do in the body, jobs no other nutrient can do. Most nutrients do their jobs best when teamed with other nutrients working in the body at the same time.

Everybody needs the same nutrients throughout life but in different amounts. Proportionately greater amounts are needed for growth in a body than just for its upkeep. Boys and men need more than girls and women. Large people need more than small people. Active people need more food energy than inactive ones. People recovering from illness need more than healthy people.

We can get all of the nutrients from foods, but no one food contains all of the nutrients. We must therefore eat a variety of different kinds of foods.

A diet that provides all the nutrients and energy in the amounts a person needs, we call a balanced diet or a well-balanced diet. Many kinds and combinations of food can form a balanced diet.

Suggestions for achieving a balanced diet are made by nutrition scientists. They translate the technical information about nutrient needs of people and the nutrient content of different kinds of food into a guide that is easy for everyone to use.

In the guide, the different foods are sorted into a few large groups on the basis of their similarity in nutrient content. Then suggestions are made for the number of servings from each food group that, with servings from the other groups, contribute to the kinds and amounts of the many nutrients needed for good nutrition—a balanced diet.

An easy guide to follow is "A Daily Food Guide" (see accompanying chart).

It gives us as wide a choice as possible among different foods while still assuring us of a balanced diet. It gives a good deal of free choice in selecting additional foods. If we are convinced of the importance of the food we eat to the way we feel, we will welcome a guide such as this one.

Many persons want to know why particular food groups are emphasized in the guide and the names of some of the important nutrients. Such information can make choosing food for ourselves and our families more rewarding.

Foods from the milk group are relied on to provide most of the mineral calcium needs for the day. They are also dependable sources of protein and contribute riboflavin and other vitamins and minerals.

Meat, poultry, fish, and eggs from the meat group are valued for the protein, iron, and the B vitamins—thiamine, riboflavin, and niacin—they provide. This is true also of their alternates, dry beans, dry peas, and nuts.

The vegetable-fruit group is depended on to supply most of the vitamin C and vitamin A value of the diet. Yet only a relatively small number of foods are really good sources of either. To protect the nutritional value of your diet, your choices are directed toward the dark-green and deep-yellow ones for vitamin A value and to citrus fruit and a few others that are among the better sources of vitamin C.

The bread-cereal group, with its whole-grain and enriched bread and other cereal products, provides protein, iron, and the B vitamins.

Fats, oils, sugars, and sweets are not emphasized in the guide because all of them are common in every diet. Some of the fats and oils provide vitamin A, and some furnish essential fatty acids, but their chief nutritional contribution is energy value.

Some persons want to know more about foods than these general groupings tell them.

They want to know the number of calories and the amounts of specific nutrients in individual foods. For them, a booklet, "Nutritive Value of Foods," is a mine of information. They will

94

find in it figures for the amounts of the key nutrients in common measures or servings of more than 500 items. Single copies can be had without charge from the Office of Information, U.S. Department of Agriculture.

From the figures in its tables we can also locate the better food sources of the key nutrients provided by a food group. For example, it would take about 1.5 ounces of Cheddar cheese, 1.5 cups of cottage cheese, or nearly 2 cups of ice cream to provide the amount of calcium in a cup of milk.

95

A fund of accurate information makes the subject of food and nutrition more meaningful to some persons—perhaps to you. That is fine.

But knowledge beyond the basic facts about your food needs is neither a prerequisite nor a guarantee to making wise food choices. A food guide can be that. Follow it. Here's to your health!

A Daily Food Guide

VEGETABLE-FRUIT GROUP

All vegetables and fruit. This guide emphasizes those that are valuable as sources of vitamin C and A.

SOURCES OF VITAMIN C—Good sources.—Grapefruit or grapefruit juice; orange or orange juice; cantaloup; guava; mango; papaya, raw strawberries; broccoli; brussels sprouts; green pepper; sweet red pepper. *Fair sources.*—Honeydew melon; lemon; tangerine or tangerine juice; watermelon; asparagus tips; raw cabbage; collards; garden cress; kale; kohlrabi; mustard greens; potatoes and sweetpotatoes cooked in the jacket; spinach; tomatoes or tomato juice; turnip greens.

SOURCES OF VITAMIN A—Dark-green and deep yellow vegetables and a few fruits, namely: Apricots, broccoli, cantaloup, carrots, chard, collards, cress, kale, mango, persimmon, pumpkin, spinach, sweetpotatoes, turnip greens and other dark-green leaves, winter squash.

CONTRIBUTION TO DIET

Fruits and vegetables are valuable chiefly because of the vitamins and minerals they contain. In this plan, this group is counted on to supply nearly all the vitamin C needed and over half of the vitamin A.

Vitamin C is needed for healthy gums and body tissues. Vitamin A is needed for growth, normal vision, and healthy condition of skin and other body surfaces.

AMOUNTS RECOMMENDED

Choose 4 or more servings every day, including:

1 serving of a good source of vitamin C or 2 servings of a fair source.

1 serving, at least every other day, of a good source of vitamin A. If the food chosen for vitamin C is also a good source of vitamin A, the additional serving of a vitamin A food may be omitted.

The remaining 1 to 3 or more servings may be of any vegetable or fruit, including those that are valuable for vitamin C and vitamin A.

Count as 1 serving: 1/2 cup of vegetable or fruit; or a portion as ordinarily served, such as 1 medium apple, banana, orange, or potato, half a medium grapefruit or cantaloup, or the juice of 1 lemon.

MEAT GROUP

Beef; veal; lamb; pork; variety meats,
such as liver, heart, kidney. Poultry and
eggs. Fish and shellfish. As
alternates—dry beans, dry peas, lentils,
nuts, peanuts, peanut butter.

CONTRIBUTION TO DIET

Foods in this group are valued for their protein, which is needed for growth and repair of body tissues—muscles, organs, blood, skin, and hair. These foods also provide iron, thiamine, riboflavin, and niacin.

AMOUNTS RECOMMENDED

Choose 2 or more servings every day.

Count as a serving: 2 to 3 ounces of lean cooked meat, poultry, or fish—all without bone; 2 eggs; 1 cup cooked dry beans, dry peas, or lentils; 4 tablespoons peanut butter.

MILK GROUP

Milk—fluid, evaporated, skim
dry, buttermilk,
Cheese—cottage; cream;
cheddar-type—
natural or processed.
Ice cream.

CONTRIBUTION TO DIET

Milk is our leading source of calcium, which is needed for bones and teeth. It also provides high-quality protein, riboflavin, vitamin A, and many other nutrients.

AMOUNTS RECOMMENDED

Some milk every day for everyone.

Recommended amounts are given below in terms of *8-ounce cups* of whole fluid milk:

Children under 9	2 to 3
Children 9 to 12	3 or more
Teenagers	4 or more
Adults	2 or more
Pregnant women	3 or more
Nursing mothers	4 or more

Part or all of the milk may be fluid skim milk, buttermilk, evaporated milk, or dry milk.

Cheese and ice cream may replace part of the milk. The amount of either it will take to replace a given amount of milk is figured on the basis of calcium content. Common portions of various kinds of cheese and of ice cream and their milk equivalents in calcium are: 1-ince cube cheddar-type cheese = ½ cup milk; ½ cup cottage cheese = ⅓ cup milk; 2 tablespoons cream cheese = 1 tablespoon milk; ½ cup ice cream = ¼ cup milk.

BREAD-CEREAL GROUP

All bread and cereals that are whole grain, enriched, or restored; *check labels to be sure.*

Specifically, this group includes: Breads; cooked cereals; ready-to-eat cereals; cornmeal; crackers; flour; grits; macaroni and spaghetti; noodles; rice; rolled oats; and quick breads and other baked goods if made with whole-grain or enriched flour. Parboiled rice and wheat may be included in this group.

CONTRIBUTION TO DIET
Foods in this group furnish worthwhile amounts of protein, iron, several of the B-vitamins, and food energy.

AMOUNTS RECOMMENDED
Choose 4 servings or more daily. Or, if no cereals are chosen, have an extra serving of breads or baked goods, which will make at least 5 servings from this group daily.

Count as 1 serving: 1 slice of bread; 1 ounce ready-to-eat cereal: ½ to ¾ cup cooked cereal, cornmeal, grits, macaroni, noodles, rice, or spaghetti.

97

OTHER FOODS

To round out meals and to satisfy the appetite everyone will use some foods not specified—butter, margarine, other fats, oils, sugars, or unenriched refined grain products. These are often ingredients in baked goods and mixed dishes. Fats, oils, and sugars are also added to foods during preparation or at the table.

These "other" foods supply calories and can add to total nutrients in meals.

Foods to Satisfy
By Mary M. Hill

We eat food to live, grow, keep well, and get energy for work and play. It is easy to learn to choose the kinds and amounts of food that help us achieve those purposes.

The daily food guide, which puts needed foods in four groups, is the beginning.

If you choose the specified amounts of food from each of the groups, you will have a good foundation, but you will want additional foods to complete your meals and to meet your need for food energy.

The number of combinations you can make is almost unlimited, so varied and abundant is our supply of food.

How much of these other foods you should eat to maintain a desirable weight will depend on your age, sex, size, activity, and state of health.

To illustrate the use of the food guide in planning the diet, I offer several examples. [*Notice* that the Food Guide does not include tea, coffee, and beer. See Chapters 5 and 8.]

Susan, 16 years old, attends a secondary school that participates in the national school lunch program. She allows little time for breakfast, but takes time to change her dress two or three times and fix her hair before she can face the world for the day.

"Breakfast makes me fat," she says, but to mollify her mother, eats a little food before she leaves for school.

Susan eats the school lunch because the students are not permitted to leave the school grounds at noon. She could bring a bag lunch from home, but her parents insist that she have a warm meal. If cake, pie, or ice cream is served, she generally substitutes a piece of fruit she brings from home. (Menus are published a week in advance.) Susan requests and receives small portions.

Susan goes with friends after school to a soda fountain. She is hungry. She feels noble because she has eaten little all day. So she splurges on an ice cream creation (793 calories).

At dinner her parents are annoyed because she eats so little— she is again worrying about her weight. At bedtime, she raids the refrigerator.

The nutritional needs of teenage girls are great, and their emotional and psychological needs are also great. A girl may suspect there is inconsistency, maybe a lack of understanding, in this.

Susan, for example, knows she should eat a balanced diet. Like most teenagers, she wants to keep a slender figure and believes mistakenly that a balanced diet will make her fat.

So Susan tries to cut down or cut out the foods that have the nutrients she needs. Then she nibbles on foods that supply little besides calories and food energy. She does not gain weight, but she shortchanges herself nutritionally.

A teenager is more apt to make better choices of food if her daily routine pattern is not seriously involved—little time for breakfast; a stop after school at the soda fountain; a late evening snack.

By following the daily food guide, Susan can meet her daily nutritional needs without altering her activities very much. She can even eat the cake, pastry, or ice cream served in the school lunch if she chooses her snacks wisely.

A day's menu for a moderately active teenage girl like Susan may be:

Breakfast—orange juice, buttered toast, and skim milk.

School lunch—salmon loaf with cream sauce, green peas, bread and butter, perfection salad (jellied vegetable) with French dressing, an apple, and whole milk.

At the soda fountain—ice cream soda.

Dinner—meat loaf, baked potato, spinach, bread and butter, cup custard, and [beverage].

Evening snack—cheese and crackers and [beverage].

If you check the food guide, you see that the suggestions for the bread-cereal group were met in the day's menu with four slices of enriched bread and four crackers eaten during the day.

Susan had four glasses of milk or milk equivalent—milk for breakfast and lunch, cream sauce for lunch, cup custard for dinner, ice cream (in the soda), and cheese in the evening snack.

Fish for lunch and meat loaf for dinner provided two servings of meat.

The four servings of vegetables and fruit were peas and apple for lunch and baked potato and spinach for dinner. The orange juice for breakfast provided the vitamin C. The spinach for dinner is one of the dark-green vegetables that are valued sources of vitamin A.

The other foods added made the meals interesting and satisfying to Susan and provided approximately the 2,300 calories of food energy a teenage girl of average activity needs daily.

A boy is different. His needs for food energy—3,400 calories for the moderately active boy—is greater than the girl's. He is not inclined to worry about his weight. He therefore eats more food and fares better nutritionally.

The food guide is a good way to check his meals to make sure he has enough of the foods included in the four basic groups.

Grandmother Caruso came to the United States some years ago, but she likes best the food she had in the old country. Her daughter-in-law, with whom she lives, cooks many of the foods that Grandmother enjoys but has added many American dishes.

Grandmother prefers spaghetti and macaroni with various meats, seafood, or cheese and served with a rich tomato sauce. She likes fruits and vegetables. If she has raw vegetables, she usually serves them with oil and vinegar. If she cooks them, they are often served with a sauce. Her meals are not complete without Italian bread and [hot beverage]. She will eat the American type prepared cereal and occasionally the milk puddings her daughter-in-law prepares for the children. When unfamiliar foods are served, however, she is inclined to make her meal of a macaroni dish, bread, and [a hot beverage].

The doctor has advised her that she should eat a greater variety of food and that she should watch her weight. He has frowned on the variety of spaghetti and other pasta dishes served with rich sauces she eats and on her preference for vegetables served with tomato and cheese sauces.

Grandmother has visions of her remaining days being filled with tasteless, uninteresting meals. The more she thinks of it, the more difficult it is to eat the food she believes she must have.

She occasionally can eat the food she enjoys, meet her nutritional needs, and keep her food energy down to the level suggested for women of her age. She will have to eat smaller portions than is her custom, however.

100

A day's menus for Grandmother Caruso may be:

Breakfast—orange juice, cornflakes, skim milk, Italian bread, enriched.

Lunch—minestrone (vegetable soup with pasta), boiled beef (from soup), Italian bread, enriched, apple, cheese.

Dinner—chicken, spaghetti, tomato sauce, mixed salad (romaine, tomato, green pepper, hard-cooked egg, oil and vinegar), Italian bread, enriched, tapioca pudding.

A check of the menus with the food guide shows that Grandmother's need for foods from the bread-cereal group were met with three slices of Italian bread and a serving of cornflakes.

An elderly person needs two cups of milk daily. Grandmother's need for milk was met with the half cup of milk . . . served with her breakfast cereal, the cheese in her lunch, and the . . . milk in the tapioca pudding at dinner.

Her need for two servings of meat was met with beef at lunch and the chicken and hard-cooked egg at dinner.

The four servings of fruits and vegetables were met with orange juice (her vitamin C need was met here), apple, the vegetables in her soup at lunch, and in her dinner salad.

These menus will supply the 1,600 calories of food energy recommended for the elderly woman. Grandmother will need to keep her portion of minestrone to 1.5 cups and her portion of spaghetti to 1 cup, served with a quarter of a 2-pound broiling chicken if she is to keep her food energy at the level of 1,600 calories.

John Doe, middle-aged, is strictly a meat-and-potatoes man. He dislikes fancy salads, especially gelatin salads, and most casserole dishes. He will eat coleslaw and occasionally a tossed green salad, but he prefers his vegetables served as such—either cooked or raw.

He enjoys food. His doctor thinks he has reached the point where he enjoys eating more than exercising. His doctor has advised him to keep an eye on his physical condition, including his weight.

The prospect of forgoing the foods he enjoys most and the [snack] in the evening as he watches the ball game on TV does not appeal to Mr. Doe. He tried cottage cheese salads with crackers and milk for lunch; he even tried the highly advertised formula diets. After a few days, Mr. Doe concluded he could not work on such food. He decided he might as well be dead as

persecuted and returned to his old pattern of eating whatever
struck his fancy without giving a thought to the food
combinations that made up his daily total intake of food.

Mr. Doe could meet his nutritional needs with foods that he
enjoys, have his occasional . . . snack in the evening, and still keep
his food energy intake to the recommended 2,600 calories for a
man of his age and activity.

A day's menus for Mr. Doe may be:

Breakfast—grapefruit, bacon and scrambled eggs, toast,
[skim milk].

Lunch—stuffed green pepper (rice and meat) with tomato
sauce, coleslaw, roll and butter, apple crisp, milk.

Dinner—swiss steak, mashed potatoes, glazed carrots, roll
and butter, coconut custard pie.

Evening snack—[beverage], crackers, and cheese.

Mr. Doe's needs for food from the bread-cereal group was
more than met with two slices of toast for breakfast, rolls for
lunch and dinner, and the rice in his lunch.

Two scrambled eggs for breakfast and swiss steak for dinner
provided the two servings of meat or meat equivalent
recommended in the guide.

Green pepper, cabbage (coleslaw), glazed carrots, and
grapefruit made up the suggested four servings of fruits and
vegetables. Grapefruit supplied the needed vitamin C and carrots
the vitamin A.

Mr. Doe got his two cups of milk or milk equivalent in the
milk he had for lunch, the custard of the pie, and the cheese in his
evening snack.

Susan, Grandmother Caruso, and Mr. Doe are illustrations
of the fact that with a reliable food pattern and a willingness to
eat and enjoy the wide variety of food available in this country,
you can eat what you need, like what you eat, and, barring
accidents, expect to live to a pleasant old age.

Selected Questions and Answers

What is meant by an adequate diet? It is one that supplies all the
known essential nutrients in sufficient amounts for the
maintenance of health in the normal individual.

Is appetite a safe guide in choosing a diet? Not necessarily. A
haphazard diet may lack certain nutrients and supply too much
of others. A satisfactory diet can be obtained from well-selected
foods in the different food groups.

What are high-calorie and low calorie foods? There is no exact line
of demarcation. The calorie value of a food depends on its
composition. In general, foods highest in calorie value are those
rich in fat and low in moisture. Other concentrated sources are

foods composed mainly of carbohydrate or protein or a mixture of either or both with fat. Sugars, cereals, dried fruits, and cheese are among the relatively concentrated sources of energy.

Foods low in calorie value in general are those that contain large amounts of water and relatively little fat. These include many fruits and vegetables, particularly succulent vegetables.

Are the same daily amounts of essential nutrients recommended for everyone? No. Needed amounts vary according to age, size, stage of growth, and condition of the individual. In general, the amounts are higher for rapidly growing boys and girls and pregnant and lactating women; they are lower for young children as well as for older persons.

Are recommended daily dietary allowances the same as minimum daily requirements? No. Recommended daily dietary allowances are amounts of nutrients that are judged to be adequate for the maintenance of good nutrition in the population of the United States. The amounts are changed from time to time as newer knowledge of nutritional needs becomes available.

Minimum daily requirements are amounts of various nutrients that have been established as standards for labeling food and pharmaceutical preparations for special dietary uses.

How does cooking affect nutrients? Some cooking procedures result in much greater losses than others. The "three R's" of cooking to retain nutrients are: Reduce the amount of water used; reduce the length of the cooking period; and reduce the amount of food surface exposed.

Is waterless cooking a superior method? Not necessarily. Although the amount of cooking water is small, the longer cooking period required by this method may offset the advantage of the smaller amount of water used.

Is pressure cooking a desirable method? This intensive method may overcook tender vegetables and result in loss of nutrients. If timing is carefully regulated, however, retention of nutrients may be as good by pressure cooking as by other methods.

Is it harmful to eat pork in summer? No. With present-day refrigeration, pork, like other meats, may be enjoyed the year around.

Is there a danger to health in raw eggs? Raw eggs are not sterile and may carry salmonella, one of the harmful bacteria. Eggs should be cooked. If the shells are cracked or badly soiled, the eggs must be thoroughly cooked.

Does cooking affect the nutrients in eggs? Only slightly.

Are white-shell eggs higher in nutritive value than brown-shell eggs? No. Color of shell is a characteristic of the breed of hen.

Is it natural for an adult to put on weight as he grows older? It may
be natural, but it is not desirable. For best health it is
recommended that a person maintain the weight that was right
for his height and body build at 25 years of age. This requires
gradual reduction of calorie intake to meet reduced energy
requirements due largely to lessening of vigorous physical
activities and decreasing metabolic rate. See Home and Garden
Bulletin No. 74, "Food and Your Weight."

Is cholesterol necessary in the body? Yes. Cholesterol, a fatlike
substance present in all animal (body) tissues, is synthesized
within the body in normal metabolic processes and is also
supplied by foods.

What is the significance of cholesterol in the diet? This has not been
clearly established. Low-cholesterol diets have received much
attention in the treatment of atherosclerosis and cardiovascular
diseases. Until more is known about the possible relationships,
however, foods should not be omitted from the diet because they
contain cholesterol.

What are the food sources of cholesterol? Cholesterol occurs only in
products of animal origin. Concentrated sources are nerve tissue,
as brains from calf, beef, lamb, hog; also egg yolk. Butter is a
relatively concentrated source. Meat, poultry, fish and shellfish,
and cheese have a fairly high content.

Some Ideas on Food Quackery

*What can be said of the so-called "health foods," "wonder foods,"
"miracle foods," "organic foods," and such?* Food quackery is of great
concern. It is often difficult for the consumer to know what is fact,
fad, or falsity among the innumerable claims made for foods. The
so-called "health foods" usually are ordinary foods.

No single food or combination of foods has any health-giving
properties other than the nutrients they provide. An ample
supply of nutrients is available from foods purchased in regular
markets at ordinary, current prices.

*What are the facts concerning the food and health values of the products
to which some writers have ascribed unusual values?* Yogurt has the same
nutritive and calorie values as the milk from which it is made.
When made from partly skimmed milk, as is often the case,
yogurt is lower in fat, vitamin A value, and calories than when
made from whole milk. It is a good source of other nutrients in
milk, particularly calcium, riboflavin, and protein.

Yogurt, like other fermented milks, has a fine curd which
may permit it to be digested more quickly than plain milk.
Yogurt has no food or health values other than those present in

the kind of milk from which it is made.

Blackstrap molasses is the third and final extraction of sugarcane and has more of the B-vitamin complex and iron, along with its impurities, than refined molasses. Blackstrap has a strong flavor, and usually only small amounts are eaten.

Brewer's yeast is a good source of the B-vitamins and of protein of high biological value. However, adequate amounts of these nutrients are present in the ordinary diet that includes meat, eggs, and whole-grain or enriched cereals.

Brewer's yeast should not be confused with baker's yeast, which is a live yeast that should not be eaten either directly or in powder form. Baker's yeast is a living organism and uses thiamine in the intestinal tract for its own growth, thus reducing the amount of thiamine from other foods that should be available to the body. Cooking renders the live property of baker's yeast inactive; in bakery products it is harmless.

Wheat germ is a part of the wheat kernel and composes 2 to 3 percent of the grain. The germ is a concentrated source of protein, iron, vitamin E, and some of the B-vitamins. It has no health-promoting qualities other than the nutrients it contributes. It is usually eaten in small amounts added to other foods.

Alfalfa leaves, like many other green leaves, are rich in carotene (a precursor of vitamin A) and in some other nutrients, but their high fiber content makes them more suitable for animal feeding than for human use. Alfalfa tea, sometimes promoted as a cure for certain disabilities, has been found in some experiments to be harmful.

Rose hips are the fruit of the rose (Rosa rugosa) and are high in ascorbic acid (vitamin C) content. When usual foods are in short supply, as in wartime, rose hips have been used in some countries to help overcome a scarcity of this nutrient. They have no unusual properties.

Sunflower, sesame, pumpkin, and squash seeds vary in nutritive value. They are relatively high in fat content and have more fiber than most foods. These seeds are used variously as appetizers, as garnish for prepared foods (sesame seed on bakery products), and in other ways. Sunflower seed is used mainly as feed for poultry. These seeds have no unique health-promoting properties.

Honey and vinegar is an imaginative combination, but these foods have no special nutritional merit, taken either singly or together. About four-fifths of the weight of honey is a mixture of sugars. The remaining one-fifth is water. Honey has only very small amounts of other nutrients. Distilled vinegar has only a trace of mineral matter.

Safflower oil has no nutrients contributing to health that are not present in various other foods. Safflower oil is higher in linolcic acid than are other fats and oils, but adequate amounts of this fatty acid can be obtained from an ordinary mixed diet of commonly used foods.

False claims that capsules of safflower oil were effective in reducing weight regardless of calorie intake and that they were effective in lowering cholesterol level of the blood and in treating arteriosclerosis and heartburn, improving the complexion, increasing resistance to colds, promoting health, and increasing sexual drive led to Government seizure of the supply as being misbranded.

105

Juices made at home (usually with well-advertised, expensive blenders) have no unusual values. On the same weight basis, juices have about the same nutritive values as the foods from which they are extracted. Juices add variety to the diet and may be useful when one is unable to eat solid food. However, juicing is a wasteful practice of both food material and nutritive value. The strained juice of an orange, for example, comprises only two-thirds to three-fourths of the edible part of the orange. Nutrients present in the pulp are lost.

What are organic foods, and are they superior in nutritive value to other foods? Organic and natural are terms that have been used by some groups to refer to foods grown in soil fertilized with only compost or manure. However, no sound scientific evidence demonstrates that such foods have nutritive values or health factors superior to foods produced with an appropriate combination of fertilizers.

Is it true that all chemicals used in the production, processing, and marketing of foods are harmful to the consumer? No. Chemicals are necessary to insure a safe, wholesome, and abundant food supply. The Federal Government has responsibility for insuring that foods in interstate commerce are safe, pure, and wholesome and are produced under sanitary conditions.

The Department of Agriculture and the Department of Health, Education, and Welfare work together on the safe use of chemicals for food products. Foods that do not meet the standards of safety and wholesomeness are seized and condemned. When a harmful residue is found on food products, they cannot be marketed. Every effort is made to label chemical products with instructions and precautions to insure safe use. It is the responsibility of every user to follow directions and heed precautions.

Homemakers should, of course, observe commonsense precautions in the home, such as washing fruits to be eaten out of hand and caring for foods in appropriate ways.

Where may information on food and nutritional quackery be obtained? Write to the Director of Information, Food and Drug

Administration, United States Department of Health, Education, and Welfare, Washington, D.C. 20201.

How may one know which books on nutrition are based on sound scientific fact and which contain false, misleading, and harmful statements? One such list is titled "Nutrition Books—Recommended and *Not* Recommended." Most of the books included in this list appeared in "Nutritional Books for Lay Readers—a Guide to the Reliable and the Unreliable" by Helen S. Mitchell, published in *Library Journal*, February 15, 1960, and in "Guide to Selected Nutrition Books," Supplement No. 1, October 1961, and Supplement No. 2, April 1962, Joint Committee on Nutrition Literature, Massachusetts Public Health Association, Boston, Mass.

A revised list, "Recommended and Non-Recommended Nutrition Books for Lay Readers," was issued in April 1964.

Inquiries about these lists may be addressed to Nutrition Section, Massachusetts Department of Public Health, 88 Broad Street, Boston, Mass., 02110; or Connecticut State Department of Health, Hartford, Conn., 06115.

Where may further information on foods and nutrition be obtained? *Food*, the Yearbook of Agriculture, 1959, is an excellent one-volume reference. For sale ($2.25) by the Superintendent of Documents, U.S. Government Printing Office, Washington, D.C. 20402. This book may be available in a nearby library. The Department of Agriculture has no copies for general distribution.

A list of popular printed publications including those on food and nutrition may be obtained from the Office of Information, U.S. Department of Agriculture, Washington, D.C. 20250. (Edna W. Soper and Bernice K. Watt, *Consumers All*, The Yearbook of Agriculture, 1965, pp. 391-416.)

Is lumpy evaporated milk safe to use? Lumps in evaporated milk are formed by the solids settling during storage. The lumps do not harm the milk. Cans of evaporated milk can be turned or shaken at frequent intervals during storage to prevent lumping.

What's a good way to lose weight? Here are a few simple rules to follow in choosing low-calorie meals:

Select a varied diet that contains the different kinds of foods important for health—milk, meat (or alternates), fruit and vegetables, and whole-grain or enriched or restored cereals and bread.

Choose the foods with fewer calories in each of these groups. For instance, skim milk and buttermilk provide fewer calories than whole milk.

Prepare and serve foods in ways that do not add calories. Avoid fried foods, rich sauces, gravies, salad dressings, rich desserts, and so forth.

Reduce the amount of food eaten.

Take smaller servings.

Avoid snacking and between-meal eating unless such foods are planned as part of the total allowance of calories.

Take some exercise regularly to increase your expenditure of calories and to keep the body physically fit.

How do I know if I am getting enough calories? Your weight is a good guide to whether you are getting enough calories. An adult should eat enough to maintain the weight that is desirable for him. Usually your weight at 25 to 30 years of age is considered your desirable weight for the rest of your life. If you weigh more than this amount, you probably are getting too many calories. If your weight is below this standard, you may need more calories. The child and teenager, who are still growing, need enough food to permit normal gains in weight. (*Food,* The Yearbook of Agriculture, 1959, p. 24, 29.)

10

Temporal Blessings
of Living the Word of Wisdom

... the word of wisdom, showing forth the order and will of God
in the temporal salvation of all saints in the last days—
Given for a principle with promise, adapted to the capacity
of the weak and the weakest of all saints, who are or can be called
saints. (D&C 89:2-3.)

When the Lord refers to temporal matters, his counsel
and instruction refer to earth-life experiences. The death of
the body is declared to be a temporal death, and the spirit
is in the likeness of the temporal body. (D&C 29:42; 77:2.)
The Word of Wisdom was given by revelation in order
that the Saints might enjoy bodily health as well as
spiritual well-being. This law pertains not only to health,
but also to other aspects of temporal welfare. From it we
learn that the Saints by obedience will receive these blessings of temporal salvation:

... health in their navel and marrow to their bones; ...
And shall run and not be weary, and shall walk and not
faint.
And I, the Lord, give unto them a promise, that the
destroying angel shall pass by them, as the children of Israel, and
not slay them. Amen. (D&C 89:18, 20-21.)

As a solution to some of the problems in the world, in
1933 President Heber J. Grant said: "Do you want to
know how to obtain temporal salvation? Not only the Latter-day Saints, but all the world would have the solution of
that problem if there were no tea, coffee, liquor, nor tobacco used in the world." (*Conference Report*, October 1933,
p. 9.)
Forty years later, in a world in which thousands of
children and adults die each year of malnutrition and starvation, a scientist's belief confirms one portion of the truth
that the gospel of Jesus Christ holds the answer to the
world's problems. Jean Mayer, Harvard University nutri-

tionist, newspaper columnist, and director of the United Nations Task Force on Children's Nutrition, announced on his return from the World Food Conference in Rome, Italy, that Americans could feed millions of starving people by limiting themselves to one drink at cocktail parties. He said that most alcohol is made from grain, and Americans drink enough beer and cocktails each year to feed 40 million to 50 million people. Then he made this statement: "It would be better for our health, it would be better for our pocketbooks, and it would be better for our consciences. The phrase, 'Have a drink and starve a child' could reduce the enjoyment of alcoholic beverages." (*Deseret News,* November 9, 1974.)

109

An economic advantage accrues to the person who obeys the Word of Wisdom by refraining from tea, coffee, tobacco, and alcoholic beverages. Promises have been made by the modern prophets that substantiate this truth. For example, President Brigham Young said: "If you observe faithfully the Word of Wisdom, you will have your dollar, your five dollars, your hundred dollars, yea, you will have your hundreds of dollars to spend for that which will be useful and profitable to you." (*Journal of Discourses,* 12:118, August 17, 1867.)

The money saved from obedience to the commandments in one year represents hundred of dollars, and when disobedience to this law continues over years, thousands of dollars are wasted without benefit to the consumer. In a few minutes one can compute his financial loss in a month or a year, and the amount is staggering when computed over an average lifetime. One computation that cannot be made immediately, except for those who know by experience, is the cost of doctor and hospital charges due to taking into one's body injurious substances.

By contrast, think of the rich benefits derived by the faithful Latter-day Saint who uses Word of Wisdom "money" in the payment of tithing and other donations to the Church.

President Grant gave hundreds of books away each year. One day a friend said:

"How can you afford to spend hundreds of dollars every year in giving books away to your friends?"

I said: "Oh, I get a great deal of pleasure out of it, and in addition I sometimes give pleasure to four or five hundred others. Sometimes I give away in a year a thousand or two thousand pamphlets that cost only ten cents each, and it is my cigar money. I am sure it does not cost me any more than you spend to gratify your own appetite in smoking cigars."

He said, "Well, you have knocked me out in the first round and with the first blow." (*Gospel Standards,* p. 248.)

Sickness and ill health teach us the blessings of enjoying the strength and power that come from a healthy body. To know the bitter in life gives us appreciation of the sweet. When ill health comes, we wish for a quick recovery. Prudence enjoined in the Word of Wisdom dictates that we prepare for good health by obedience to this law. Every righteous man and woman desires to raise a posterity that will bring honor to his name and to give to their children the best advantages in life.

The expression "health in the navel" has meaning in terms of the health and well-being of one's children. The umbilical cord joining the mother and her unborn child provides nourishment during the growth of the baby, and, importantly, determines to some extent how healthy that baby will be as it begins life's journey. Children inherit much from their progenitors, especially from their parents. Those whose parents are healthy and free from contaminating habits have greater possibilities for desirable physical traits and mental capacity. Science is now finding that some drugs when taken during the formative stages of the embryo can result in serious genetic abnormalities. Improper nutrition of the mother during pregnancy and even during her entire lifetime may have an important influence on her unborn child, emphasizing the desirability of adhering to the positive aspects of the Word of Wisdom.

Section 89 of the Doctrine and Covenants uses the phrase "marrow to their bones." From the time of birth and even before, marrow performs a necessary function in the maintenance of good health. Two kinds of marrow are necessary for good health. Yellow marrow consists of blood vessels, fat cells, and fibre, while red marrow manufactures blood cells to replace those destroyed daily and by infection, anemia, and loss caused by accidents and illnesses associated with hemorrhage. The process of building and rebuilding blood cells is a continuous one. If poisons are continually being assimilated, the capacity to provide sufficient red corpuscles is diminished and anemia may result.

111

President Brigham Young counseled the Saints not to trifle with their mission in life by indulging in the use of injurious substances. These contribute to the foundation of disease and death, which includes "insufficient" bone, sinew, muscle, and physical constitution. He reminded the Saints that anciently people lived hundreds of years and raised the question, ". . . where is the iron constitution, the marrow in the bone, the power in the loins, and the strength in the sinew and muscle of which the ancient fathers could boast?" (*Journal of Discourses,* 12:118, August 17, 1867.)

To run and not be weary and to walk and not faint, as mentioned in section 89 of the Doctrine and Covenants, means that physical endurance is received by those who will observe not only the "don'ts" but also the "do's" of the Lord's law of health.

President David O. McKay gave this counsel to young men, counsel that applies to all who desire to have physical stamina:

> To boys I would say, that if they want to live physically, if they want to be men strong in body, vigorous in mind, if they want to be good sports, enter the basketball game, enter the football game, enter the contest in running and jumping, if they want to be good Scouts, if they want to be good citizens, in business, anywhere, avoid tobacco and live strictly the religious life. I am not afraid to call it the religious life to them. It is not a thing that will make them gloomy and sad. Live the gospel of Jesus Christ, for it is the science of life revealed from on high. (*Gospel Ideals,* p. 362.)

Gene Tunney, former heavyweight boxing champion

of the world, gave his counsel to all potential smokers, the young, and others, while he was in charge of physical training and athletics for the U.S. Navy:

112

> To me the ugliest of advertising is that which features soldiers or sailors smoking cigarettes. As Director of the Navy's Physical Fitness Program, I can bluntly say that few things could be worse for physical fitness than promoting the cigarette habit.
>
> Sentimentalists will object: "Why deprive the boys of the innocent pleasure of tobacco?" My reply is: "Should our citizen army be less rigidly conditioned than a college football team?" And here's a special word to mothers—send your boy in camp athletic equipment instead of cigarettes—a baseball mitt or a set of boxing gloves.
>
> If you think this sounds goody-goody, take a look at my companions in the nonsmoking section. The late Knute Rockne, Notre Dame's wonder coach, said: "Tobacco slows up reflexes, lowers morale; any advertising that says smoking helps an athlete is a falsehood and a fraud." William Muldoon, famous conditioner of men, considered nicotine the greatest harm to health in the modern world. Ty Cobb, the famous Georgia Peach of baseball, says: "Cigarette smoking stupefies the brain, saps vitality, undermines health and weakens moral fiber. No one who hopes to be successful in any line can afford to contract so detrimental a habit." (Gene Tunney, "Nicotine Knockout, or The Slow Count," *Improvement Era,* January 1942, p. 53.)

Although it happened some years ago, the experience of Paul C. Kimball, Rhodes Scholar at Oxford University, is a good example of what obedience to abstaining from the "dont's" of the Word of Wisdom can do for young men engaging in athletic contests. In a public discourse he told of the time at Oxford University when he was asked to coach in rowing a group of inexperienced young men. He received from each one the promise that they would not use tea, coffee, tobacco, or alcoholic beverages. In competition with fifty crews from other colleges, some of whom were experienced in the sport of rowing, his crew kept up with the leaders for the first half of the race. Then, when he called for them to sprint, within a minute they had stretched out a hundred feet ahead of the nearest competitor, and they finished the race three hundred feet ahead. When asked how this feat was accomplished by such a young, inexperienced crew, he replied:

> I made those boys live right. I made them cut out tobacco, alcohol, tea, and coffee. When the sprint came, their lungs were clean; their systems were clean; their blood was clean, and their nerves were strong. ("The Word of Wisdom in Practical Terms," extracts from an address delivered in the Salt Lake Tabernacle, May 24, 1931.)

113

Heart disease is one of the major causes of death and incapacity in the United States. Granted that this disease may be caused in other ways than through breaking the Word of Wisdom, it has been established that heart disease may result from use of tobacco. Dr. Wilbert S. Aronow, cardiologist, has said:

> Most people are aware that cigarette smoking is a primary cause of cancer of the lung. Fewer are aware of the link that joins smoking and heart disease.
> Many studies, both prospective and retrospective, have shown that cigarette smoking is a significant risk factor contributing to the development of coronary disease, especially in young and middle-aged men. ("Tobacco and the Heart," *Journal of the American Medical Association,* September 23, 1974.)

Dr. Aronow added that some heart disease patients have a significant decrease in exercise performance.

The destroying angel mentioned in the twenty-first verse of the Word of Wisdom revelation may be interpreted as death, but in its literal sense there are angels of destruction who have left the portals of heaven and are waiting to "reap down the wheat with the tares," said President Wilford Woodruff in 1894. He prophesied that the next twenty years would see great changes among the nations of the earth, for calamities would increase—and this statement was made just twenty years before the start of World War I. President Woodruff also said, "If you do your duty, and I do my duty, we'll have protection, and shall pass through the afflictions in peace and safety." (*Young Women's Journal,* August 1894, pp. 512-13.)

When Pharaoh of Egypt would not release the Israelites at Moses' command, and this despite the numerous plagues that visited the land, the final plague, with the "destroyer" taking the firstborn of each Egyptian family, finally brought the Israelites' release. They were protected because they obeyed the Lord's instruction that they strike the lintel and sideposts of their houses with the blood of a lamb. (See Exodus 12:21-23, 30.)

114

The Lord's instruction to Latter-day Saints is to keep his commandments, including the Word of Wisdom, that they may receive the blessing of protection from the plagues and sicknesses of the last days. (See D&C 89:21.)

A fundamental question was posed by President George Q. Cannon, counselor in the First Presidency, on the experience of the Israelites:

> Suppose the children of Israel, after receiving that direction from the Lord through the Prophet Moses, had either refused or neglected to sprinkle the doorstep and lintels with blood, could they have reasonably expected the promise to be fulfilled to them? Certainly not. And why should people in our day expect to enjoy health and an exemption from the visit of the destroyer when he goes forth as he did in Egypt if they do not comply with the conditions which the Lord has prescribed? (*Juvenile Instructor,* November 15, 1892, pp. 689-91.)

The promise of health and protection does not insure an everlasting life in mortality. All men must die. (See 1 Corinthians 15:22; 2 Nephi 9:6.) Meaningfully, President J. Reuben Clark, Jr., gave the following interpretations:

> But it does mean that the destroying angel, he who comes to punish the unrighteous for their sins, as he in olden times afflicted the corrupt Egyptians in their wickedness, shall pass by the Saints, who . . . "remember to keep and do these sayings." These promises do mean that all those who qualify themselves to enjoy them will be permitted so to live out their lives that they may gain the full experiences and get the full knowledge which they need in order to progress to the highest exaltation in eternity, all these will live until their work is finished and God calls them back to their eternal home, as a reward.
>
> These blessings will come to those who qualify as sure and certain as life itself. (*Conference Report,* October 1940, pp. 18-19.)

In testimony of the Lord's promises to the faithful, Elder Rudger Clawson of the Council of the Twelve said:

Let me say here, in all solemnity, that those who fail to keep this law cannot justly claim the promise.

I fancy I hear some one say: "Ah, Brother Clawson, my father was a good man, a faithful Latter-day Saint. He kept the commandments of God, he was an observer of the Word of Wisdom. At the age of seventy he died, and the destroying angel came and took him away."

My answer to that is: "Brother, would you make the promise of God of non-effect? Would you intimate that the Lord who gave this law and this promise unto his people failed in your father's case to keep his promise? Surely it was not so. True, the angel of death may have been in your father's home when he passed away, in fact may have come for your father, but he was not a destroying angel, no, he was an angel of peace, of mercy, of hope, of love, and he came to open the door of light and life and everlasting joy to your good father."

Death comes to all. The death of the righteous is sweet but the death of the wicked, of the rebellious, of those who are wilfully neglectful of their duty and treat lightly the sacred commandments of God, is bitter. [D&C 42:46-47.] (*Conference Report,* April 1925, p. 62.)

11

Spiritual Blessings
by Obedience

And all saints who remember to keep and do these sayings,
walking in obedience to the commandments . . . shall find
wisdom and great treasures of knowledge, even hidden treasures.
(D&C 89:18-19.)

The gospel of Jesus Christ consists of many teachings
given by revelation. The Lord has never counseled anyone
to ignore or neglect any divine commandment. He has always admonished his people to live strictly by the revelations of his mind and will. It is only the disciple of the Lord
Jesus Christ—one who accepts fully the commandments
and seeks to incorporate them into his life—who will be
saved eternally. (See D&C 41:5-6.)

Wonderful are the blessings to be received by the faithful, for theirs will be the fulness of knowledge—"all the
hidden mysteries of my kingdom from days of old, and for
ages to come." (D&C 76:7.) It is as inconsistent to believe
that obedience to one or a few laws of the gospel will bring
omniscience as it is to believe that all men will eventually
receive the same kingdom in the eternal worlds following
the resurrection. (D&C 76:5-6, 50-70.) By keeping the commandments, one is cleansed from all sins. (D&C 76:52.)

Blessings come to the person who lives a law of the
gospel, but the fulness of blessings comes to him who lives
the *laws* of the gospel. He who abstains from tea, coffee, tobacco, harmful drugs, and alcoholic beverages will receive
the benefits of bodily health. He who abides by the positive
points of this law—eating foods that give nourishment—
will also benefit physically. However, the major blessings
from obedience to this commandment, as to all commandments, are spiritual.

President Stephen L Richards of the First Presidency
gave the following evaluation of the Word of Wisdom:

Every commandment of God is spiritual in nature. There are

no carnal commandments. We have learned this from modern revelation. [D&C 29:34-35.] While the commandments have effect upon the body and temporal things they are all in essence spiritual. The Word of Wisdom is spiritual. It is true that it enjoins the use of deleterious substances and makes provision for the health of the body. But the largest measure of good derived from its observance is in increased faith and the development of more spiritual power and wisdom. Likewise, the most regrettable and damaging effects of its infractions are spiritual, also. Injury to the body may be comparatively trivial to the damage to the soul in the destruction of faith and the retardation of spiritual growth. So I say, every commandment involves a spiritual principle. (*Conference Report*, April 1949, p. 141.)

117

Spiritual laws or commandments are rules of conduct from God, the violation of which brings penalties, while obedience thereto brings communion with God in this life and eventual godhood.

Law is absolute in its blessings and penalties. If one does not abide by the law of the celestial kingdom, he may not receive a place in that realm where God the Father and Christ dwell. (D&C 88:22.) When one governs his life by divine law, he becomes perfected and sanctified by the law. To break the law and become a law unto oneself is sin, and such a person cannot be "sanctified by law, neither by mercy, justice, nor judgment." (D&C 88:34-35.) On the other hand, he who lives the law is justified by God because he cleaves unto principles that bring him nearer to God. (D&C 88:39.)

For intelligence cleaveth unto intelligence; wisdom receiveth wisdom; truth embraceth truth; virtue loveth virtue; light cleaveth unto light; mercy hath compassion on mercy and claimeth her own; justice continueth its course and claimeth its own; judgment goeth before the face of him who sitteth upon the throne and governeth and executeth all things. (D&C 88:40.)

There is a difference between the individual who sins and the one who strives diligently to refrain from sinning. President Charles W. Penrose declared:

If we do evil, evil impressions come naturally, and if we love to do good, a good influence, a good spirit, is with us, and round about us, and in our being and we are sustained and supported thereby; and if we are corrupt and wicked and abominable and rebellious, the effects of our acts are right in our nature, and these things will be disclosed just as naturally as the opening of books made of paper and written upon with ink. (*Conference Report*, April 1917, p. 18.)

118

When a person breaks the law of God, he sins. The enormity of such an act may not appear to be serious to one who has not attuned himself to God's Spirit, and it may take the form of remarks such as these: "I do not want to be deprived of the privilege of taking a little, if I want it. When I think it is going to do me good, I want to take it." "A little alcohol does not harm anyone." "I don't believe that the Lord will punish me for drinking tea and coffee."

President David O. McKay once told of some correspondence he received that revealed a point of view that persists to some extent today:

> "Would it not be better," writes one, "if the elders said less about the Word of Wisdom, and preached more about love, repentance, and the consequences of sin?"
>
> The answer to this is very simple. These, they ought to teach, but not leave the other untaught. Neither the Church nor the world at large can hear too much about the Word of Wisdom. It is a doctrine given to man for man's happiness and benefit. It is a part of the philosophy of living. It should be observed not only by every elder, but also by every member of the Church. The elder who hesitates to teach it is shirking his duty. He who fails to live it robs himself of strength of body and strength of character to which he is entitled. Truth is loyalty to the right as we see it; it is courageous living of our lives in harmony with our ideals; it is always power. With the ideals of right living before him, no Latter-day Saint can continually violate the Word of Wisdom with impunity. (*Gospel Ideals*, p. 377.)

In a general conference message, President Spencer W. Kimball said: "Those who break the Word of Wisdom have strange and spurious excuses for using of these obnoxious things. How can anyone ignore the revelations given through a living prophet? The Lord reiterated it through another prophet and made it a definite commandment." (*Conference Report*, October 1974, pp. 5-6.)

The usual meaning of wisdom is sound judgment, the

power of judging rightly based on knowledge, understanding, and experience. The Psalmist declared that the fear of God is the beginning of wisdom, and he who has it keeps the commandments of God. (Psalm 111:10.) A Book of Mormon prophet also equated wisdom with keeping the commandments of God while in one's youth. (Alma 37:35.) These divine truths bring to us the important fact that he who seeks divine knowledge and directs his life thereby possesses wisdom. The Word of Wisdom is true knowledge, knowledge from God that has been verified scientifically and in the crucible of experience, as demonstrated by the experiences of hundreds of thousands of Latter-day Saints. That person who obeys the injunctions of this revelation is wise for many reasons, one of which is that he might develop wisdom to a great degree. The Lord has said: "Seek not for riches but for wisdom, and behold, the mysteries of God shall be unfolded unto you, and then shall you be made rich. Behold, he that hath eternal life is rich." (D&C 6:7.) Wisdom brings joy and happiness, and "wickedness never was happiness." (Alma 41:10.)

These words of wisdom from the Prophet Joseph Smith give the essence of true knowledge and the letter and spirit of the gospel of Jesus Christ: "I . . . spoke to the people, showing them that to get salvation we must not only do some things, but everything which God has commanded. . . . It mattereth not whether the principle is popular or unpopular, I will always maintain a true principle, even if I stand alone in it." (*History of the Church of Jesus Christ of Latter-day Saints,* 6:223.)

Unless one has as his object in life the keeping of the commandments to insure salvation in the presence of God and exaltation in the celestial kingdom, his sights are not in accord with God's wisdom, for his purpose is to "bring to pass the . . . eternal life of man." (Moses 1:39.) Consequently, the Lord's instruction to those who wish to receive exaltation is to walk "uprightly before me, considering the end of your salvation, doing all things with prayer and thanksgiving, that ye may not be seduced by evil spirits, or doctrines of devils, or the commandments of men; for some are of men, and others of devils." (D&C 46:7.)

The Lord has said that he gave the Word of Wisdom "in consequence of evils and designs which do and will exist in the hearts of conspiring men in the last days." (D&C 89:4.) The enticings of devils and of men are those which place before the youth and adults things that encourage the breaking of God's commandments.

The purpose of Satan and his cohorts is to work for the debasement and ultimate degradation of mankind. If they can entice, persuade, and accomplish the downfall of a son or daughter of God, their nefarious mission is accomplished. Every inducement to break divine commandments paves the way for their ultimate victory. What results from breaking the Word of Wisdom? From Elder George A. Smith of the Council of the Twelve we learn:

> I notice in the observance of the Word of Wisdom, a manifestation of the Holy Spirit connected with it. Whenever a person has failed to observe it, and becomes a slave to his appetite in these simple things, he gradually grows cold in his religion; hence, I constantly feel to exhort my brethren and sisters, both by precept and example, to observe the Word of Wisdom. We should not be thoughtless, careless, nor neglectful in the observance of its precepts. (*Journal of Discourses*, 14:212, August 13, 1871.)

What greater victory could Satan desire than to keep people from praying, to increase their disobedience to God's laws, and to eventually apostatize from the Church?

What are some of the effects of disobedience to the Word of Wisdom that keep one from possessing spirituality, the Spirit of the Lord? Read what President Heber J. Grant said:

> . . . the use of liquor and tobacco is one of the chief means in the hands of the adversary whereby he is enabled to lead boys and girls from virtue.
>
> Nearly always those who lose their virtue, first partake of those things that excite passions within them or lower their resistance and becloud their minds. Partaking of tobacco and liquor is calculated to make them a prey to those things which, if indulged in, are worse than death itself. (*Gospel Standards*, p. 55.)

120

Living the Word of Wisdom will not always protect one from immorality, but keeping all of the commandments, including the Word of Wisdom, is the sure way to ensure the presence of the Lord's Spirit.

The Word of Wisdom promises those who observe it fully "great knowledge." In the context in which the adjective *great* is used in the expression "great knowledge," it means much higher in degree, above the average; a synonym is *grand*, meaning "most important." What is the most important knowledge that one can acquire in life, after having learned, as a child, the rudiments of means much higher in degree, above average; a synonym is *grand*, meaning "most important." What is the most important knowledge that one can acquire in life, after having learned, as a child, the rudiments of knowledge? It is the knowledge that saves one eternally in the kingdom of God. (See D&C 131:6; 130:18-19.) It is the knowledge found in the standard works—the Bible, Book of Mormon, Doctrine and Covenants, and Pearl of Great Price, plus the sermons and writings of the prophets, seers, and revelators!

From the life-giving words of the prophets, we learn to be obedient to the laws of salvation; we understand the reason for each of the commandments; we grow in faith and power. President Joseph Fielding Smith said that the Saints must

121

endeavor to acquaint themselves with the gospel, that they shall receive line upon line, precept upon precept, here a little and there a little, until the fulness of truth shall be their portion; even the hidden mysteries of the kingdom shall be made known unto them: "For every one that asketh receiveth; and he that seeketh findeth; and to him that knocketh it shall be opened." [Matthew 7:8.] All these are heirs of salvation, and they shall be crowned with glory, immortality, and eternal life, as sons and daughters of God, with an exaltation in his celestial kingdom. (*Doctrines of Salvation*, 1:303.)

Think of it! Knowledge—testimony—spiritual strength—physical vigor and immunity from the destroying angel! Remember also that here comes protection from that more deadly destruction:

"And fear not them which kill the body, but are not able to kill the soul; but rather fear him which is able to destroy both body and soul in hell." (Matt. 10:28.) (Spencer W. Kimball, *Conference Report*, April 1952, p. 23.)

122

Elder Boyd K. Packer of the Council of the Twelve reminded youth, in a general conference message, that the so-called successes of those in business, motion pictures, and politics have ofttimes been received by indulgence in things contrary to the Word of Wisdom. But, he said,

> Your opportunity is not so much in what you will contribute materially but in the influence that you may have spiritually. . . .
> You, my young friends, can be sensitive to inspiration and spiritual guidance. To do this you need the wisdom and treasures of knowledge—they constitute a spiritual confirmation, your testimony of the truth. To have this witness fulfills the promise of the Lord. To be denied it is the penalty. (*Conference Report*, April 1963, p. 108.)

President Spencer W. Kimball once answered the question, "Is success in learning secular knowledge the same as success in acquiring spiritual knowledge?"

> To have both the secular and spiritual is the ideal. To have only the secular is like Jude said: ". . . clouds they are without water, carried about by winds; trees whose fruit withereth." (Jude 12.)
> Desirable as is secular knowledge, one is not truly educated unless he has the spiritual with the secular. The secular knowledge is to be desired; the spiritual knowledge is an absolute necessity. We shall need all of the accumulated secular knowledge in order to create worlds and to furnish them, but only through the "mysteries of God" and these hidden treasures of knowledge may we arrive at the place and condition where we may use that knowledge in creation and exaltation. (*Conference Report*, October 1968, p. 131.)

What are the "hidden treasures" promised to those who keep the commandments of the Lord? Hidden knowledge of great value may be the answer to this question, but the knowledge must be available to the faithful member of the Church in order for him to enjoy it and for it to serve him in his journey to eternal life. This knowledge is hidden from the world except as the world receives the means by which it is attainable—acceptance of the fulness of the gospel through The Church of Jesus Christ of Latter-day Saints. However, the world in general will not receive the gospel because of wickedness, a part of which is due to the use of substances contrary to God's law. (See D&C 45:28-29.) President David O. McKay taught that the peril of this century is spiritual decay, which is far greater than physical decay.

> As the body requires sunlight, good food, proper exercise, and rest, so the spirit of man requires the sunlight of the Holy Spirit; proper exercise of the spiritual functions; avoiding of evils that affect spiritual health, which are more ravaging in their effects than typhoid fever, pneumonia, or other diseases that attack the body. (*Gospel Ideals*, p. 360.)

President Spencer W. Kimball has related an experience of Don B. Colton, former U.S. Representative from Utah, that illustrates the meaning of "hidden treasures." Congressman Colton taught a Sunday School class in Washington, D.C., and was asked by a university student why Latter-day Saint students are not academically ahead of students who do not observe the Word of Wisdom. He could not answer the question fully that day, but during the following week, he had an experience that provided the answer. He was lunching with several congressmen, and when some commented on the fact that he drank neither liquor nor coffee and that he did not smoke, one Congressman who had attended an LDS fast and testimony meeting came to his defense:

> This church service was different. I had never seen one like it. A man called the bishop conducted the meeting. The singing was by the congregation, the prayer by a man from the audience, apparently called without previous notice. Soft music was played. All was silent as one young man knelt and said a prayer over bread which he and his companion had broken into small pieces, and then several boys, probably twelve or thirteen years of age, took plates of broken bread and passed it to the congregation. The same was done with little cups of water. After the choir sang an anthem, I expected to hear a sermon, but the bishop announced, "Brothers and sisters, today is your monthly fast and testimony service, and you may proceed to speak as you feel led by the Spirit. This time is not for sermons, but to speak of your

own soul and your inner feelings and assurances. The time is yours. . . ."

Never before had I experienced anything like this. From the congregation people arose. One man in a dignified voice said how he loved the Church and the gospel and what it meant in the life of his family.

124   From another part of the chapel a woman stood and spoke with deep conviction of a spectacular healing in her family as an answer to prayer and fasting, and closed with what the people called a testimony—that the gospel of Jesus Christ as taught by the Church was true; that it brought great happiness and a deep peace to her.

Still another woman arose and bore witness of her sureness that Joseph Smith was truly a prophet of God and had been the instrument of the Lord in restoring the true gospel of Christ to the earth.

A man from the choir, evidently a recent immigrant, seemed sensitive about his language. He was struggling with his v's and w's and verbs and sentence construction. Two years ago, two young missionaries in faraway Holland had taught him the restored gospel. He told how happy his family had been since embracing it and what a transformation had come in their lives.

The old and the middle-aged and the youth responded. Some were farmers and laborers and there were teachers and business and professional men. There was no ostentation, no arrogance, but a quiet dignity, a warm friendliness, a sweet spirituality.

Then came in succession several children. They spoke less of their knowledge of spiritual things but more of their love for their parents and for the Savior, of whom they had learned much in Primary and Sunday School and at home.

Finally the bishop stood and in a few appropriate words of commendation, expressed his own sureness. Then he closed the meeting. . . .

Never had time passed so rapidly. I had been entranced. And as each additional speaker had concluded in the name of Jesus Christ, I was moved, deeply stirred, and I pondered: How sincere! How sweet and spiritual! How sure these people seem to be of their Redeemer! How much at peace! What security they have in their spiritual knowledge; what strength and fortitude, and what purposeful lives! (Spencer W. Kimball, *Faith Precedes the Miracle,* Deseret Book, 1972, pp. 275-76.)

The Congressman then added:

I thought of my own children and grandchildren and their helter-skelter existence, their self-centered activities, their seeming spiritual vacuums, their routine lives in search of wealth and fun and adventure. And I said to myself with an enthusiasm new to me, "How I wish my own posterity could have this sureness, this faith, this deep conviction. Why, these humble people seem to have a secret that most people do not enjoy; something worth more than all else—a hidden treasure of spiritual wholeness." (Ibid., pp. 276-77.)

125

The following Sunday Elder Colton was prepared to tell his Sunday School class that the "hidden treasures" promised in the Word of Wisdom revelation came from the Holy Spirit, giving knowledge that would, if lived, bring eternal life in the celestial world.

The whole plan of salvation in the restored gospel consists of doctrine, principle, and teaching that is hidden to the uninformed. On several occasions, Jesus spoke of knowledge hidden from the world, but known to his disciples only. (See Matthew 11:25; 13:10-13.) The answers to such basic questions as Who am I? Why am I here? What is my potential destiny after death?—these and others are found in the fulness of the gospel and constitute knowledge of great worth to every person. This kind of knowledge, hidden treasure, must be earned by one's diligence in keeping the commandments.

Elder LeGrand Richards of the Council of the Twelve sums up this discussion of the worth of great treasures of knowledge:

Is there any treasure of knowledge in this world to be sought after, more desirable than to know that God lives, that Jesus is the Christ, to know that his kingdom has been established again in the earth, to know that God has promised a reward for every commandment that he has given, to know that he has created this earth that we might prove unto him that we would do all things, not just a few of them, all things whatsoever the Lord our God hath commanded? (*Conference Report*, April 1961, p. 46.)

12

A Summary of
the Word of Wisdom Today

Perhaps one of the most distinguishing features of the Church is the fact that its people abstain from liquor, tea, coffee, and tobacco. Of course, there are some who apparently have not the courage nor the testimony to follow this program, but numerous thousands observe it strictly. (Spencer W. Kimball, *Conference Report*, October 1974, p. 5.)

It [the Word of Wisdom] is God's law of health, and is binding upon each and every one of us. We cannot escape its operation, for it is based upon eternal truth. Men may agree or disagree about this word of the Lord; if they agree, it adds nothing; if they disagree, it means nothing. Beyond his word we cannot reach, and it is enough for every Latter-day Saint, willing and trying to follow divine guidance. (Statement of the First Presidency, October 1943.)

The Church of Jesus Christ of Latter-day Saints was organized by divine commandment received through the Prophet Joseph Smith on April 6, 1830. Before this date and subsequent thereto the Prophet received revelations for the organization and direction of the Church and also for the salvation of those who would join its ranks. By and large, these revelations are compiled in the Doctrine and Covenants, the opening revelation being the "Preface." Among other things the Lord commands all people to hearken to his words of warning, admonition, and counsel for their eternal salvation. (D&C 1:1-4.) He says:

Search these commandments, for they are true and faithful, and the prophecies and promises which are in them shall all be fulfilled.

What I the Lord have spoken, I have spoken, and I excuse not myself; and though the heavens and the earth pass away, my word shall not pass away, but shall all be fulfilled, whether by mine own voice or by the voice of my servants, it is the same.

For behold, and lo, the Lord is God, and the Spirit beareth record, and the record is true, and the truth abideth forever and ever. Amen. (D&C 1:37-39.)

"In consequence of evils and designs which do and will exist in the hearts of conspiring men in the last days," the Word of Wisdom was given to protect members of the Church from products fostered on the public by those whose love of money exceeds their love of mankind. Specifically, tea, coffee, tobacco, and alcoholic drinks are mentioned in the revelation as injurious, "not good for man." Scientific information regarding these deleterious things was unavailable to the Saints when the revelation was received February 27, 1833, but through the years, especially in the twentieth century, considerable research has verified the truth of the Lord's commandment, and we are confident that additional research will further confirm that these harmful products are not good for man.

The Word of Wisdom not only commands the Saints to abstain from injurious things, but also establishes the fact that there are foods that are "best for man." The philosophy of the gospel of Jesus Christ holds that earth life is the period when God's spirit sons and daughters, tabernacled in bodies of flesh and bones, are to receive their opportunity to be proved to see if they will, amid life's temptations, keep the commandments of God. The gospel teaches that man should respect his body, knowing that it is God-given, and he will have it forever and ever as a resurrected being, having the same materials out of which it was created by mortal birth. The apostle Paul said our bodies are the holy temples of God in which the Spirit of God may dwell. (1 Corinthians 3:16-17.)

A healthy body is the proper tabernacle for the spirit of man, which is born in a premortal world, and should not be defiled by things from which we should abstain; furthermore, a healthy body is not maintained simply by abstinence from harmful products. For this purpose the Lord has informed us that we should eat vegetables and fruits in The season thereof, defined as high vitamin-carrying products, a truth not scientifically known in 1833 but discovered about seventy-five years later. All grains, especially wheat, are good for man, a fact that is also verified today. Meat is to be used sparingly.

Although the Word of Wisdom was given soon after the Church was organized, the Lord was merciful in not condemning those who did not fully subscribe to its provisions. Concerning the hard environment in which the early Latter-day Saints lived, especially after the Church moved to the West, Elder John A. Widtsoe wrote:

128

> In those frontier settlements food was usually plentiful but seldom of the best variety. Meat predominated; grains were usually available; vegetables and fruits were scarce. For stimulation resort was often had to home-brewed alcoholic beverages, though there was little or no drunkenness; to tobacco, mostly for chewing; and to tea and coffee. These substances were commonly and freely used when available. This, of course, did not give permanent relief from the pains of the body, which were due in large part to the lack of correct physiological knowledge. (*Joseph Smith, Seeker After Truth, Prophet of God,* Bookcraft, 1951, p. 198.)

"Not by commandment or constraint" are the words that seemed to justify the laxness of many in that early period in the application of the Word of Wisdom. However, those who lived it because it was given as "the order and will of God in the temporal salvation of all saints in the last days . . . adapted to the capacity of the weak and the weakest of all saints, who are or can be called saints," with a promise, realized its blessings in their lives.

Under the inspiration of the Lord, President Brigham Young enjoined upon the Saints obedience to this law. It had been received as a commandment, but old habits, hard to discontinue, made it difficult for the leadership of the Church to bring strict obedience to this revelation. Even today there are many who have fallen prey to the enticings of Satan. The Lord gave the Saints many years in which to bring themselves into harmony with his will. Presidents of the Church through the years continued to admonish obedience to the Word of Wisdom and the other commandments. It was President Heber J. Grant, seventh president of the Church (1918-1945), who brought the Church membership to a recognition that this law must be lived. Among his statements relative to this subject are:

I have urged upon the people, and have been called a crank for so doing, the observance of the Word of Wisdom and I expect to continue to be a crank in that respect to the end of my life. I am converted beyond the shadow of a doubt that no man or woman in this Church who does not observe the Word of Wisdom can grow and increase in a knowledge and testimony of the gospel as he or she could otherwise do. (*Gospel Standards* , p. 249.)

I would like it known that if we as a people never used a particle of tea or coffee or of tobacco or of liquor, we would become one of the most wealthy people in the world. Why? Because we would have increased vigor of body, increased vigor of mind; we would grow spiritually; we would have a more direct line of communication with God, our Heavenly Father. (Ibid., p. 50).

The Lord has said that though he refers to temporal laws, no commandment given by him is temporal only, but all commandments are spiritual. (D&C 29:34-35.) President Joseph F. Smith emphasized the importance of this principle, saying that if religion cannot save people temporally, it cannot exalt them in worlds to come. (Albert E. Bowen, *The Welfare Plan,* p. 36.)

Among the temporal blessings received from living the health laws of the Word of Wisdom are protection of the unborn child, a healthy body after birth, physical endurance, long life, and freedom from the plagues of the last days. And what of those who fail to keep these laws? Here are some statements from latter-day Church leaders regarding their fate:

One of the most conspicuous of our indignities comes through the use of alcoholic beverages. Is there anything more pitiable than men and women who have lost their senses in drunkenness?

Observe any intoxicated person; listen to his babbling. Does liquor improve his opportunity of becoming an heir of God and a joint heir with Jesus Christ?

Liquor can only lower the dignity and honor and respectability of man. Any effort to make it more available aids and abets the moral breakdown that always accompanies intoxication.

I ask you frankly, is there anything Christlike in it? Would your Savior encourage you to make liquor any more available than it already is? (Mark E. Petersen, *Conference Report,* October 1968, p. 101.)

We deplore the practice of many business and professional firms and others who serve liquor as a part of the entertainment in their special parties. We are especially concerned that at 130 Christmastime many celebrate this holy birth of Jesus Christ our Lord with a so-called social hour which surely must be an affront to him. Is it not a sad reflection upon people to have a drink to have a good time, or to take a stimulant to give them energy or self-assurance? (Spencer W. Kimball, *Conference Report,* October 1974, p. 6.)

In answer to the question "Why do men stupefy themselves with tobacco?" Gene Tunney said:

I have never heard a sensible reply. But let me tell you the story of the Bedouin chief who told the young men of his tribe: "There are three good reasons for smoking: First, if you smoke enough tobacco, you smell so strong the dogs will never bite you. Second, if you smoke long enough, you will develop a lung trouble which will make you cough even when you sleep. Robbers hearing you cough will think you are awake and so will not try to steal your belongings. Third, if you smoke as much as you can, you will have many diseases, and will die young." ("Nicotine Knockout, or The Slow Count," *Improvement Era,* January 1942, p. 53.)

Self-mastery is a virtue to be prized by all. Slavery to appetite binds one to habit-forming drinks that take away the user's freedom, while control over appetite develops a moral force necessary to live fully the other commandments. President David O. McKay said:

Obedience to the Word of Wisdom develops greater spiritual power, that spiritual power which comes from resistance. . . . Be master, not a slave. Look around you and see the slaves to appetite—unfortunately now, increasingly among women— slaves! Where is the spiritual power in these future mothers? (*Gospel Ideals,* p. 398.)

The letter of the Word of Wisdom regarding other commandments is: "And all saints who remember to keep and do these sayings, *walking in obedience to the commandments,* shall receive blessings. . . ." (D&C 89:18; italics added.)

Elder Ezra T. Benson said:

When we first heard the revelation upon the Word of
Wisdom many of us thought it consisted merely in our drinking
tea and coffee, but it is not only using tea and coffee and tobacco
and whiskey, but it is every other evil which is calculated to
contaminate this people. The Word of Wisdom implies to cease
from adultery, to cease from all manner of excesses, and from all
kinds of wickedness and abominations that are common amongst
this generation—it is, strictly speaking, keeping the
commandments of God, and living by every word that
proceedeth from His mouth. (*Journal of Discourses,* 2:358, April 8,
1855.)

131

President Joseph Fielding Smith wrote:

Now if we want to become heirs, joint-heirs with Jesus Christ,
possessing the blessings of the kingdom, there is only one thing
required of you and of me, and that is that we keep the *whole law,*
not a part of it only. Do you think it would be fair, just, proper,
for the Lord to say to us: "I will give unto you commandments;
you may keep them if you will; you may be indifferent about the
matter if you will; keep some, reject others; or, partially keep
some; and I will punish you, but then I will make it up to you,
and all will be well." (*Doctrines of Salvation,* 2:37.)

In the Sermon on the Mount, the Savior discourses on
false prophets and gives the standard for their teachings: as
"a corrupt tree bringeth forth evil fruit," and "a good tree
bringeth forth good fruit, . . . wherefore, by their fruits ye
shall know them." (See Matthew 7:15-20.)

Notwithstanding the fact that not all members of the
Church observe the Word of Wisdom, the vital statistics of
the Church over the years are commendable. In the state of
Utah, where the population is predominantly Latter-day
Saints, from 1900 to 1944 the death rate for Latter-day
Saints was lower for each ten-year period.

Since 1948, when the highest death rate (6.37) was
recorded in the Church since 1940, the rate has, with a few
exceptions, gradually decreased until in 1973 there were
4.74 deaths per thousand. On the other hand, the *Statistical
Abstract of the United States* indicates that in 1947 the death
rate per thousand in the United States was 10.1 and since
then it has ranged between 9.2 and 9.7. The difference

between the death rate of the Church and that of the United States is significant.

Recently a brief report was released titled "Strikingly Low Cancer Mortality Among Mormons," by Dr. James E. Enstrom of the School of Public Health at the University of California at Los Angeles. The report, noting that 73 percent of Utah's population is Latter-day Saint, stated:

132

> The Mormons are interesting from an epidemiological standpoint because their "Word of Wisdom" forbids the use of tobacco, alcohol, coffee, tea, and addictive drugs. Their religion also stresses a well-balanced diet, particularly the use of wholesome grains and fruits, and moderation in the eating of meat. One could reasonably expect Mormons to experience a low incidence of and death from various cancers, similar to that observed in the Seventh-day Adventists. (*UCLA Cancer Bulletin*, April/May 1974, p. 1.)

In comparing data on death rates due to cancer in the United States and Utah, it was found that "the cancer rates and total mortality rates for Utah are the lowest in the United States. Also, the 1970 per capita consumption of cigarettes, liquor, wine, and beer in Utah is approximately 50% of the corresponding consumption of California and the United States, and is the lowest in the entire country. This data on the amount of smoking and drinking might account for the lower mortality in Utah." (Ibid., p. 5)

The Human Population Laboratory of the California State Department of Health made a study in 1965, with subsequent follow-up of 6,928 adult residents of Alameda County, California. The percent of Latter-day Saints in the sample who neither drank liquor nor smoked was much smaller than that of others included in the survey:

> . . . the Mormons have a total mortality rate which is about 55% of the rate for the total sample during the 6 1/2 year follow-up period. The biggest difference in habits between Mormons and the total sample occurred among regular church attenders, where essentially 100% of the Mormons do not smoke or drink. Additional results from this study show that Mormons are similar to the total sample in most other respects, including socioeconomic status and medical care. (Ibid.)

In a study using 1970 records of Church members in California and Utah, a comparison of age-adjusted cancer death rates per 100,000 was made with United States records, with the following results: males in the United States (white), 153, and females, 106; California (white) males, 152, and females, 107; Utah (white) males, 109, and females, 80; California Latter-day Saint males, 74, and females, 66. In commenting upon these data, Dr. Enstrom writes:

133

The ratio of observed to expected mortality is about one-half of all causes of death and for all cancer sites, and substantially less than one-half for several sites, although the statistical errors are large for the rarer cancer sites. Particularly interesting is the low ratio for sites such as stomach, colon, rectum, breast, uterus, prostate, kidney, and lymphomas. Most of these cancers have never been clearly related to any risk factors, such as smoking. The observed number of cancer deaths has been converted into an age-adjusted mortality rate and compared [with] . . . similar rates for the California, Utah, and United States white populations. This comparison is noteworthy because the Mormons appear to have the lowest cancer rate of any group of Americans studied, with the possible exception of the Seventh-day Adventists [who also "abstain from the use of tobacco and alcohol and to a lesser extent from meat, fish, coffee, and tea"]. (Ibid.)

Although he recognized the fact that 40 percent of the California Latter-day Saints studied were converts whose life-style before joining the Church may have been quite different, and assuming that "environmental carcinogenic factors primarily exert their influence early in life," Dr. Enstrom said:

Thus active life members who faithfully live by the Church regulations may have substantially lower mortality rates than those discussed above for Mormons as a whole.

Further study will attempt to determine exactly what components of the Mormon life style are related to their extremely low death rates. Several possibilities are: low consumption of tobacco, alcohol, coffee, tea, soft drinks, and drugs; dietary habits; religiosity; and general health practices, including exercise and proper sleep and weight. Elucidation of previously undiscovered factors protective against cancer could have considerable implication for cancer control and prevention. (Ibid.)

Concerning other fruits of the gospel, a study conducted in 1960, "Utah's Comparative Position in Education," concluded: "Historically, Utahns have placed a great amount of emphasis on education. A number of impartial studies over the years have placed Utah at or near the top in overall educational performance." (Utah Foundation Research Report, Number 171, February 1960.) In a summary of a National Education Association report, titled *Rankings of the States, 1963,* Utah ranked first among the fifty states in percent of Selective Service registrants passing the mental test in 1961; first in percent of population twenty-five years old and older with more than eight years of schooling; and first in percent of population twenty-five years old and older with at least four years of high school in 1960.

Though factors other than the Word of Wisdom alone may contribute to the desire and drive to become educated, including the gospel truth that men are not saved in ignorance, Latter-day Saints should never forget this evaluation by President Heber J. Grant:

> No man who breaks the Word of Wisdom can gain the same amount of knowledge and intelligence in this world as the man who obeys that law. I don't care who he is or where he comes from, his mind will not be as clear, and he cannot advance as far and as rapidly and retain his power as much as he would if he obeyed the Word of Wisdom. (*Conference Report*, April 1925, p. 10.)

President Joseph Fielding Smith said:

> If we have a failing, if we have a weakness, there is where we should concentrate, with a desire to overcome, until we master and conquer. If a man feels that it is hard for him to pay his tithing, then that is the thing he should do, until he learns to pay his tithing. If it is the Word of Wisdom, that is what he should do, until he learns to love that commandment. (*Conference Report*, October 1941, p. 95.)

If a person requires knowledge of the revelation's truth, he should seek for that confirmation through sincere

134

prayer. If he needs help in overcoming a habit contrary to the Word of Widsom, the Lord will give him sufficient strength to set the habit aside, provided he will diligently try to overcome it.

How blessed are those who keep the commandments of the Lord! They reap the blessings of a clear conscience, mental and physical health, and the Spirit of the Lord, which enlightens their minds and their hearts in receiving "wisdom and great treasures of knowledge, even hidden treasures."

135

And moreover, I would desire that ye should consider on the blessed and happy state of those that keep the commandments of God. For behold, they are blessed in all things, both temporal and spiritual; and if they hold out faithful to the end they are received into heaven, that thereby they may dwell with God in a state of never-ending happiness. O remember, remember that these things are true; for the Lord God hath spoken it. (Mosiah 2:41.)

Bibliography

Articles, Bulletins, Periodicals, Miscellaneous

Better Feeding of Livestock, U.S. Department of Agriculture Farmers Bulletin No. 2052, U.S. Government Printing Office, Washington, D.C., 1952.

Call, Richard A., M.D., "Tissue Damage from Alcohol." (Unpublished speech.)

Church News, weekly supplement to the *Deseret News*.

Conference Reports, proceedings of annual and semiannual conferences of The Church of Jesus Christ of Latter-day Saints, Salt Lake City, Utah.

Consumer Bulletin, April 1971.

Consumer Reports, January 1971.

Deseret News, Salt Lake City, Utah.

Drug Intelligence and Clinical Pharmacy, December 1974.

Ensign, Salt Lake City, Utah.

"False and Misleading Advertising," *Twentieth Report by the Committee on Government Operations*, U.S. Government Printing Office, Washington, D.C., 1958.

Feed Situation, U.S. Department of Agriculture, Washington, D.C., November 1968.

Field, S. S., "Nicotine: Profile of Peril," *Reader's Digest*, September 1973. Reprinted with permission from the *Reader's Digest*; copyright © 1973 by Reader's Digest Association, Inc.

Improvement Era, Salt Lake City, Utah.

Johnson, Joel H., *Voice from the Mountains*, pamphlet in the Harold B. Lee Library, Brigham Young University, Provo, Utah.

Journal History, The Church of Jesus Christ of Latter-day Saints, Church Historical Department, Salt Lake City, Utah.

Journal of the American Medical Association, September 23, 1974.

Journal of Discourses, Salt Lake City, Utah.

Juvenile Instructor, Salt Lake City, Utah.

Medical Bulletin on Tobacco (for Physicians) American Public Health Association, American Heart Association, American Cancer Society, and National Tuberculosis Association, April 1968.

Millennial Star, Liverpool, England.

Modern Medicine.

Mooney, Hugh J., "What the Cigarette Commercials Don't Show," condensed from *Christian Herald; Reader's Digest*, January 1968. Used by permission.

New England Journal of Medicine.

New Era, Salt Lake City, Utah.

Ochsner, Alton, "Tobacco and Cancer of the Lung," a forum assembly address at Brigham Young University, May 20, 1959. Extension Publications, BYU, Provo, Utah.

Pageant, December 1950.

PTA Magazine, May 1973.

Science Digest, October 1963; July 1966.

Swine Production, U.S. Department of Agriculture Farmers Bulletin No. 1437, U.S. Government Printing Office, Washington, D.C., 1958.

Times and Seasons, Nauvoo, Illinois.

Today's Health, April 1967.

UCLA Cancer Bulletin, vol. 1, no. 4, April/May 1974.

Young Women's Journal, Salt Lake City, Utah.

Books

Bowen, Albert E., *The Church Welfare Plan,* Salt Lake City: Deseret News Press, 1946.

Brown, Norma C., *The Alcohol Question,* Cincinnati, Ohio: Standard Publishing Co., 1943.

Consumers All, The Yearbook of Agriculture, 1968.

Dobyns, Fletcher, *The Amazing Story of Repeal,* Chicago: Willett, Clark & Company, 1940.

Doxey, Roy W., *The Doctrine and Covenants and the Future,* Salt Lake City: Deseret Book Co., 1972 (rev.).

_____, *The Doctrine and Covenants Speaks,* 2 vols., Salt Lake City: Deseret Book Co., 1964, 1970.

_____, *The Latter-day Prophets and the Doctrine and Covenants,* 4 vols., Salt Lake City: Deseret Book Co., 1963-65.

_____, *Prophecies and Prophetic Promises from the Doctrine and Covenants,* Salt Lake City: Deseret Book Co., 1969.

Draper, John C., M.D., *A Textbook on Anatomy, Physiology and Hygiene,* New York: Harper and Brothers, 1866.

Food, The Yearbook of Agriculture, 1959.

Food for Us All, The Yearbook of Agriculture, 1969.

Free, Joseph P., *Archaeology and Bible History,* Wheaton, Illinois: Scripture Press Book Division, 1956.

Grant, Heber J., *Gospel Standards,* comp. G. Homer Durham, Salt Lake City: Deseret News Press, 1941.

Health Consequences of Smoking, A Public Health Service Review: 1967.

Health Consequences of Smoking, A Report to the Surgeon General: 1971.

Health Consequences of Smoking, A Public Health Service Review: 1973.

Health Consequences of Smoking, A Report to the Surgeon General, 1972.

McConkie, Bruce R., *Mormon Doctrine,* Salt Lake City: Bookcraft, Inc., 1958.

McKay, David O., *Gospel Ideals,* Salt Lake City: Improvement Era, 1953.

Oaks, L. Weston, *The Word of Wisdom and You,* Salt Lake City: Bookcraft, Inc., 1958.

Ochsner, Alton, *Smoking and Cancer, A Doctor's Report,* New York: Julian Messner, Inc., 1954.

Pickett, Deets, *Some Notes on the Alcohol Problem,* New York: Abingdon-Cokesbury Press, 1947.

Smith, Joseph F., *Gospel Doctrine* (6th ed.), Salt Lake City: Deseret Book Co., 1943.

_____, *Church History and Revelation,* Salt Lake City: Deseret News Press, 1949.

_____, *Doctrines of Salvation,* vols. 1-3, Bruce R. McConkie, comp., Salt Lake City: Bookcraft, Inc., 1954-56.

Smith, Joseph Fielding, comp., *Teachings of the Prophet Joseph Smith,* Salt Lake City: Deseret Book Co., 1938.

Smoking and Health, Report of the Advisory Committee to the Surgeon General of the Public Health Service, 1964.

Talmage, James E., *The Articles of Faith,* Salt Lake City: Deseret Book Co., 1950.

Widtsoe, John A., *Joseph Smith, Seeker After Truth, Prophet of God,* Salt Lake City: Bookcraft, Inc., 1957.

Widtsoe, John A. and Leah D., *The Word of Wisdom, A Modern Interpretation,* Salt Lake City: Deseret Book Co., revised edition, 1950.

Index

141